CURATED TRUE CRIME

FAMILY ANNIHILATORS

MURDER, MADNESS AND MAYHEM
BOOK 3

JAMIE MALTON

AIDEN GALWAY

MP

Malton
Publishing
LLC

MaltonPublishing.com

ISBN 978-1-959137-24-5

WORD OF WARNING

THE DETAILS WRITTEN in these stories come directly from eyewitness accounts, interviews, court transcripts, crime scenes, and autopsy reports. Due to the graphic nature of the crimes featured in *Curated True Crime* which include: murder, domestic violence, sexual assault, hate crimes, sex work, incest, mental illness, child abuse, animal abuse, abduction, suicide, mutilation, and necrophilia, reader discretion is advised.

GET A FREE BOOK, AND MORE . . .

1. As a thank you to my readers, I created a special volume of my other series *Killer Case Files: 20 All New True Crime Stories.* You can download it right now for FREE at this link. https://dl.bookfunnel.com/tf4q1gethc

2. Would you like to join my **Launch Team** and receive a free volume before it's published?

If you are a reviewer on any of the well-known platforms like Amazon, Goodreads, or Instagram, you could receive an advance review copy of my future volumes. I'd love to have you on my official launch team!

More Info Here

3. To see all of my books - including multi-volume bundles and boxed sets - visit my Amazon author page here. My Author Page

4. Start Reading my *Killer Case Files: 100 Shocking Stories of Murder and Mayhem* bundle right here!

Killer Case Files Bundle

Thank you for being a reader.

Sincerely,

Jamie Malton

INTENTIONAL

Twelve-year-old Devonte Hart came into the national spotlight when a photograph of him crying while hugging a police officer during a 2014 protest went viral. This image became known as the "hug felt 'round the world." The photograph, showing Devonte, a young African-American child, and Sergeant Bret Barnum in riot gear locked in a heartfelt hug, happened in the wake of a Missouri grand jury's decision not to indict a Ferguson police officer in the fatal shooting of Michael Brown.

Seeing Devonte holding a sign that read *Free Hugs*, Sergeant Barnum approached him, extended his hand for a handshake, and engaged him in conversation. Moved by the young boy's vulnerability, the police officer expressed his regret, uttering a simple "I'm sorry" in response to Devonte's obvious pain. Their exchange continued, and Barnum, pointing to the sign Devonte held, asked if he, too, could receive one of those much-needed embraces.

Standing nearby, a young photographer, Johnny Nguyen, recognized the moment's significance and caught it on his camera. Johnny, who had also shared a hug with Devonte that day, initially thought he would share the photograph on his personal Instagram account, but instead, he approached the newspaper, *The Oregonian*, who bought the rights to publish it. At the time, Johnny asked Devonte's mother, Jennifer Hart, who also attended the protest, about the child's tears. Hart said her son Devante just had a huge heart.

From that point forward, the photograph took on a life of its own. Within days, it had been shared on social media hundreds of thousands of times. The image subsequently reached prominent platforms like Reddit, ABC News, Fox News, and NBC's *Today* show.

However, the attention garnered by this evocative image was not without its consequences. The Hart family, thrust into the spotlight, found themselves overwhelmed and subjected to a barrage of positive and negative reactions. Amidst the outpouring of support, they also received disturbing death threats via email. Jennifer Hart expressed her fear of being recognized and targeted in public, leading her to make the difficult decision to relocate her family from Oregon to Washington for more privacy.

Jennifer Hart and her wife, Sarah, both grew up in South Dakota. Jennifer was from Huron, while Sarah was from Big Stone City. Born in the same year, 1979, both women were the eldest children in their families, Jennifer having two siblings and Sarah three.

Jennifer and Sarah began their romantic relationship at Northern State University in Aberdeen, South Dakota. Their academic pursuits focused on elementary education, and both wanted to work with children. Sarah graduated in 2002, but Jennifer left the university without completing her degree.

In 2005, a significant development took place in their lives. Sarah petitioned a local court to change her last name to Hart to match Jennifer's. Four years later, in 2009, they traveled to Connecticut to get married, as same-sex marriage was not yet recognized in all U.S. states.

Once they were married, the Harts distanced themselves from their own families, and the couple's early life was marked by a struggle for acceptance. On Facebook, Jennifer described how they initially hid their relationship while living in South Dakota. When they came out as a same-sex couple, they experienced a loss of friends. In 2004, they relocated to Alexandria, Minnesota, where both women found employment at a Herberger's store, and they chose to be open about their relationship. Jennifer would later become a stay-at-home mom in 2006, while Sarah ascended to a managerial position at Herberger's.

FOSTERING AND ADOPTION

Before trying to adopt children, Jennifer and Sarah Hart had served as foster parents to a 15-year-old girl. However, they abruptly ended this arrangement, leaving the girl at a therapy session to be informed by the therapist that the Harts would not be returning for her.

The first three children to be adopted by the Harts in 2006 were Abigail, Hannah Jean, and Markis. The children were adopted from Colorado County, Texas. A year after this adoption, the Harts expanded their family further by adopting three additional children, Ciera, Devonte, and Jeremiah, all originally from Houston.

The adoption of the latter three children was fraught with complications. Their biological mother, Sherry Davis, had lost custody due to substance abuse problems. The children were then placed with their paternal aunt, Priscilla Celestine, under the condition that they have no contact with their biological mother. However, violating this condition led to the children being removed from Celestine's care and put into foster care. Their older brother, Dontay, was not adopted by the Harts due to behavioral issues. As a teenager, Dontay had already spent time under psychiatric care for bipolar disorder, and the Harts felt he would be too dangerous to adopt. While living in Minnesota, the Harts received funds from the state of Texas for the children, which accounted for almost half of their total family income.

Jennifer Hart, who was particularly active on social media, used Facebook to project an image of a loving, happy family.

"I am a better human in every possible way for knowing these children. They have been my greatest teachers. Contrary to the common notion that we can't choose our family, we absolutely can. We choose by loving — and that's worth celebrating every damn day."

JENNIFER HART, FACEBOOK

Because the family consisted of two white same-sex mothers and six African-American children, her posts often touched upon race, politics, and how her family had transcended these issues. This online facade of harmony and happiness obscured some of the harsh realities developing within the family.

ACCUSATIONS OF ABUSE

In 2008, a teacher noticed bruises on Hannah's arm, and Hannah told her teacher that Jennifer had hit her with a belt. Within months of this incident, the Harts took all the children out of the public school system for a year. In 2010, Abigail reported having "owies" on her back and stomach, expressing her fear of the Harts, who she claimed had beaten her and held her head under cold water over a stolen penny. These accusations led to an inquiry from authorities about the welfare of the children. When confronted, all the children claimed they had been regularly spanked and deprived of food. Sarah took responsibility for the abuse and claimed her temper got out of hand. She was charged with domestic assault and malicious punishment. She agreed to plead guilty to the domestic assault charge, and the malicious punishment charge was dropped. Sarah was sentenced to a year of community service.

The Hart family moved from Minnesota to West Linn, Oregon, where the abuse continued. In 2013, Oregon authorities were made aware of new abuse claims. They decided to speak to the children individually and interview people who knew the family. Two family friends revealed that the children were forced to raise their hands before speaking, were not allowed to wish each other a happy birthday, and could not laugh at the dinner table. Other troubling reports suggested the children were underfed and appeared small for their ages.

Despite these disturbing observations, the children did not disclose any new incidents of abuse during their interviews. When questioned, Jennifer attributed the family troubles to intolerance towards their unconventional family. The investigation concluded, and authorities could not definitively determine whether there was a safety threat to the children.

After the national exposure and threats from Devonte's photo with the police officer in Portland, the family moved again, this time settling near Woodland, Washington. Here, Sarah took up another managerial position at Kohl's department store in Hazel Dell, Washington.

HELP FROM NEIGHBORS

An alarming incident occurred in August 2017 when Hannah, in a desperate escape attempt, jumped out of her second-story bedroom window in the middle of the night and ran to her neighbors, the DeKalbs. She pleaded with them, "Don't make me go back! They're racists, and they abuse us!" Her plea was ignored when the Harts got her and took her back home. They explained to the DeKalbs that Hannah was lying and the children were "drug babies" who suffered from emotional problems.

Following this event, the DeKalb family began interacting more with the children, especially Devonte, who would beg them for food. Devonte asked the DeKalbs to leave food in a box in their yard once a day. Devonte would retrieve the food and share it with his brothers and sisters. He begged the DeKalbs not to tell their mother, Jennifer, about the food. Devonte told his neighbors that his adoptive mothers used food deprivation as punishment and that the children were sometimes physically abused. This, coupled with Hannah's previous escape attempt, prompted the DeKalbs to report the Harts to the police and the Washington State Department of Social and Health Services. Caseworkers tried twice over the next week to reach the Harts, but the women continued to evade the consequences of their actions for a while longer.

MURDER-SUICIDE

On March 26th, 2018, Jennifer and Sarah Hart committed a horrifying act. In a calculated act of murder-suicide, Jennifer steered their family vehicle, a GMC Yukon XL, over a 100-foot cliff into the Pacific Ocean in Mendocino County, California.

The aftermath of the crash was a grim scene. The bodies of five of the children—Hannah, 16, Markis, 19, Jeremiah, 14, Abigail, age 14, and Ciera, age 12—were discovered either in or near the vehicle, which had landed upside down in shallow water below the cliff. The medical examiner's report showed older bruising on Abagail's body, not sustained in the crash, and Ciera's body only consisted of a foot inside a tennis shoe. The body of 15-year-old Devonte was never found. However, a superior court judge ruled that Devonte was in the vehicle at the time of the crash, and a death certificate was signed in his name.

An in-depth analysis of the vehicle's internal airbag-deploying computer provided chilling insights into the moments leading up to the crash. The Yukon had been intentionally driven off the cliff's edge from a standing stop, accelerating to 20 mph in just three seconds with the throttle pushed to 100%. The computer showed the Yukon took three seconds to fall into the ocean below.

Jennifer's blood alcohol content was over the legal limit at the time of the crash. Additionally, both Sarah and two of the children had diphenhydramine, an over-the-counter antihistamine that can cause drowsiness, in their systems. During the death investigation, Sarah's Google search history revealed chilling inquiries about the lethality of Benadryl. Other search phrases were, "Is death by drowning relatively painless?" And "How long does it take to die from hypothermia in water while drowning in a car?" Another search included "No-kill shelters for dogs," indicating a plan for the family's two dogs, later found alive inside the Hart family home.

Despite the murderous act, the California Highway Patrol stated that criminal prosecution was not possible due to the deaths of all responsible parties. The case was officially closed by the Mendocino County Sheriff's Department.

Dontay Davis, the older brother of Ciera, Devonte, and Jeremiah and the only sibling not adopted by Sarah and Jennifer Hart, was in a Texas prison serving three years for robbery when the murders happened. He found out about the death of his siblings upon his release six months later.

A TOWN OF CELEBRATION

Celebration is a meticulously planned community near the Walt Disney World Resort in Osceola County, Florida. It was conceived as a Utopian city inspired by Walt Disney's vision and was developed as part of Walt Disney World's expansion. The community features residential areas, office spaces, schools, a health care center, and a downtown district. The architectural design of each structure and home was meant to create a small-town atmosphere within its 4,900 acres. Each house built had to align with a Disney-created pattern book, ensuring uniformity in the structure and color of the homes. Over time, the community was criticized for its fictional town look portrayed in movies like *The Stepford Wives* and *The Truman Show*. The first family moved into the Celebration community on June 18th, 1996, and all was well for a while.

In 2010, Celebration saw its first homicide. Matteo Patrick Giovanditto was found strangled with a shoelace and hacked with an ax in the Disney planned community. The investigation into Giovanditto quickly revealed that the victim was a monster. Giovanditto was a pedophile who had sexually abused boys across the US. In recent years, his victims were students at a private Jewish school in Miami Beach where he taught. Many young boys at the Lehrman Community Day School came forward with stories of child sex abuse.

Giovanditto had asked a 30-year-old man, David-Israel Murillo, to wash his car and offered to pay him in beer. Once the task was finished, Murillo fell asleep in Giovanditto's condo. When he awoke, the man was on top of him, sexually assaulting him. Murillo found an axe in the condo and used it on Giovanditto before finally strangling him. Murillo was eventually caught and convicted of the murder and sentenced to life in prison. While this was the first murder in Celebration, it would not be the last.

Anthony Todt was only four years old when he watched a young man enter his home in Bensalem, Pennsylvania, and shoot his mother in the head. Anthony's father, Robert, had hired a former student to murder his wife, intending to free himself to marry his 17-year-old mistress. Miraculously, Loretta survived the attack but lost vision in one eye and retained the bullet in her skull. Her husband Robert was convicted in 1981 of attempted homicide, criminal conspiracy, and criminal solicitation for hiring a hitman and served 10 years in prison. Loretta, who initially believed in her husband's innocence, divorced him and later remarried.

As an adult, Anthony, living in Connecticut, married Megan Gula, a fellow physical therapist and a yoga instructor. They met during college and later established a shared physical therapy clinic. When the couple had their children, Megan became a stay-at-home mother while Anthony managed their clinic.

The Todts were a well-regarded family in their community. The children Alek, Tyler, and Zoey were encouraged to engage in arts and music, while Anthony often volunteered as a youth soccer coach and worked with disabled children. However, the family dynamic shifted in 2017 when, according to Anthony, Megan contracted Lyme Disease from a tick bite during a trip to Disney World. The disease led to bouts of depression, causing Megan to become more reserved and isolated.

Life took another turn when the Todt family relocated from Connecticut to Celebration, Florida. Anthony continued his work at the clinic in Connecticut, visiting his family in Florida weekly. In contrast to their active community involvement in Connecticut, the Todts became withdrawn in Celebration. By 2019, Anthony's health had begun to deteriorate. He had gained a significant amount of weight and was diagnosed with diabetes.

FRAUD INVESTIGATION

In April 2019, a secret came to light when it was discovered that Anthony was defrauding his physical therapy patients in Connecticut, charging them for care they had never received. An initial investigation by authorities revealed that he had used the extra money to pay rent on the family's second residence in Celebration and to finance trips to Disney World for the family. He had also taken out additional loans from banks in New York City to keep his physical therapy practice afloat. Anthony had over $100,000 in debt and owed $6000 in back rent on his Celebration home.

CHRISTMAS IN CELEBRATION

The Todts broke their usual tradition of returning to Connecticut to enjoy the winter snow, choosing instead to remain in Celebration, Florida, for the season. Despite the presence of the Todts in their home, mail began to accumulate on the porch unopened. By this time, the landlord of the home had filed the paperwork to evict the family, and a 30-day eviction notice was posted on the door of the Celebration home.

Two weeks before Christmas, Anthony's sister in Connecticut received a text message from Megan Todt's phone that said all the children were sick. The message also referenced the "coming apocalypse." The sister wrote back but received no response. She became concerned when neither Anthony nor Megan would answer their phone and called police several times. Finally, on December 29th, police performed a welfare check on the Todt residence but received no response from inside the house.

A warrant was issued for Anthony's arrest in the fraud investigation, and police returned to the house to arrest him. They found Anthony wandering in the yard, muttering and walking strangely. With a key obtained from the landlord, authorities entered the Todt residence and were immediately struck by a foul odor. Police officers walked through the house and discovered the bodies of Megan Todt and her three children in the various bedrooms. Each body showed signs of stab wounds to the abdomen, and Megan and the two boys, Alex, 13, and Tyler, 11, had crucifixes in their hands. Four-year-old Zoe Todt's body was at first overlooked due to the advanced state of decomposition. She was eventually found beneath the feet of her mother's corpse. Adding to the grim scene, the family dog, Breezy, was found lifeless on the floor in her bed in the master bedroom.

Anthony Todt was arrested for fraud on the scene and later was charged with four counts of first-degree murder and one count of animal cruelty. He had ingested a large amount of Benadryl in what he claimed later was a suicide attempt, which accounted for his odd behavior on arrest. The same drug was also found in the children's bodies, suggesting they had been drugged before their deaths.

The motive behind the gruesome murders committed by Anthony Todt remains shrouded in mystery. It is believed that Megan and the children were oblivious to the fraud, as they were not involved in the day-to-day business. Anthony's recorded confessions shifted multiple times, adding layers of confusion to an already complex case. At one point, Anthony claimed that Megan had taken her own life and those of their children, stabbing herself in the liver after murdering each child. According to Anthony, Megan, who suffered from depression, had fed the kids pie laced with Benadryl and Tylenol. In a different account, he said Megan stabbed herself, and he ended up smothering her. He then stabbed and smothered all of the children and the dog. He painted himself as a man trying to spare his family from an impending apocalypse. His Benadryl overdose was an attempt to join them in the afterlife.

At trial, the prosecutor, Danielle Pinnell, tried to clarify to the jury what really happened to the Todt family. According to her, Anthony Todt went into his daughter Zoe's bedroom shortly before Christmas and rolled on top of her until she suffocated. He then went into Alek's bedroom and suffocated and stabbed the boy in the abdomen. Tyler was sleeping on a sofa downstairs, and Anthony again suffocated the child and stabbed him in the stomach. It was unclear if Anthony stabbed Megan or she stabbed herself, but he ended up smothering her with a pillow. According to the prosecutor, Anthony also suffocated Breezy, the dog.

Anthony Todt took the stand in his own defense and claimed he was "10000% innocent of all these preposterous charges." He said he wanted to correct all of the "inaccuracies from various media outlets," and he was ready to file multiple lawsuits as soon he got out of custody.

In 2022, Anthony Todt was sentenced to life in prison without the possibility of parole. But the court took an additional step, setting a legal landmark. Recognizing the act of killing the family pet as one of animal cruelty, the court added an extra year to his sentence for the death of Breezy.

THE COMING STORM

In February of 2011, Colonel Parker Schenecker, an Army intelligence officer, was sitting at his desk in Qatar. He had just returned from a quick deployment in Afghanistan and was getting ready for his next mission when two officers, an Army colonel and an Air Force captain in battle dress uniforms, came to his office door. Initially, Parker thought they were his new teammates for the next mission, but when he saw their somber look, he knew that something was terribly wrong before they even spoke.

The officers explained that his daughter, 16-year-old Calyx, and his son, 13-year-old Beau Schenecker, were found dead at his house in Tampa Bay, Florida and that his wife, Julie, had been arrested on suspicion of their murder. Devastated, Colonel Schenecker spent the next 17 hours on a trip back to the United States to plan funerals for his children.

Julie Powers Schenecker was born in 1961 in Muscatine, Iowa. She and Parker Schenecker had met in Germany during the 1980s, a time when the world was still mired in the Cold War. Julie was working as a Russian linguist, a role critical in the geopolitical landscape of the time. Their meeting abroad eventually led to marriage, children, and a life built together in Tampa, Florida.

THE INITIAL INVESTIGATION

When Parker arrived home, he learned more of the details surrounding the murders of Calyx and Beau. His wife had allegedly shot Beau from the side at point-blank range in the family car on the way back from soccer practice. Julie then went inside the house and shot their daughter Calyx from behind as she was sitting in front of her computer doing her homework. The police told Parker their deaths were quick, and they didn't believe the children knew their mother meant to harm them.

The officers told Parker that Beau had been shot twice with a .38 revolver and was found in the family's garage covered with a blanket. Officers found his sister, Calyx, in her bed, also covered with a blanket. Julie Schenecker was discovered unconscious on the rear porch of the house, her body smeared with blood.

Upon regaining consciousness, Julie confessed to the police that she had killed her children because they "talked back and were mouthy." A chilling note in Julie's journal was discovered in the house, outlining a premeditated plan to murder her children and commit suicide. She had purchased a gun five days before the murder and wrote a note to her husband after she murdered the children.

"Tues. Feb 1st. Beau is in the van…Calyx is in her bed. Tried to make her comfortable…I believe I've saved them from the pain. I wish this on nobody… You didn't teach the kids to be compassionate… Neither were you. I sense a divorce is inevitable. I can't live alone."

Julie Schenecker was admitted to Tampa General Hospital in the immediate aftermath of the tragic events. The reasons behind her admission remained obscured, but she was released the next day. On release, Julie was charged with two counts of first-degree murder, and just over a week after the murders, a grand jury formally indicted her. Aided by her legal counsel, she entered a plea of not guilty. Her defense team indicated to the judge their intention to pursue an insanity defense. The prosecution initially announced that they would seek the death penalty for Julie, but they later declined to do so.

MENTAL HEALTH ISSUES

Julie had suffered from mental health issues for more than two decades. She was diagnosed with depression and was on daily medication from 1997 to 2001. She also suffered from severe postpartum depression after the birth of her son Beau. In 2001, she was hospitalized for nine months for severe depression, and Parker had to hire a nanny to care for the children. She was diagnosed later with bipolar disorder and schizoaffective disorder. In 2010, she had several surgeries, which left her addicted to Oxycontin. At one point, she was using Oxycontin and alcohol together, and Parker forbade her from driving the car with the children.

Several months before the murders, the Tampa police had visited the Schenecker home following an allegation of child abuse made by Calyx, the older of the two children. The police report, while not leading to charges, did contain an unsettling detail: Julie Schenecker acknowledged that she had hit her daughter.

Calyx had confided this during her weekly therapy sessions, recounting that her mother had struck her in the face after a cross-country practice on November 2nd, 2010. The therapist reported the allegation to the police, and when investigators visited the home four days after the reported incident, they found no visible injuries on Calyx. According to the police report, Calyx told investigators that her mother had "hit her with an open hand on her face for approximately 30 seconds". These details, while disturbing, did not lead to any charges against Julie.

Family and friends were concerned in the weeks leading up to the murders of the children. Parker addressed some of the issues in a group email exchange less than a month before the murders.

"I appreciate your concern about our current situation. For those of you who have committed to help by both showing up at our home to lend a hand and those of you who have committed to be here immediately if there's a problem we can't handle, I will forever be in your debt. But for those critical of this handling of the current crisis, or how I parent my children, I appreciate your concern. And no worries, I'll write off your criticism as ignorance.

Have you ever lived with someone with bipolar disorder? Did you stay in that relationship or leave? If you stayed, you have my utmost respect, and I'd appreciate your insight on how best to deal with the daily uncertainty and unpredictability and the exhaustion that it brings.

Have you ever lived with a 50-year-old who has the judgment of a 10-year-old? Did you stay in that relationship, or did you leave? If you stayed, you have my utmost sympathy. And I appreciate your insight on how to explain it to your kids and keep it from negatively affecting them and others.

Have you ever had to deal with your spouse hitting you in front of your children? Have you ever had to deal with your spouse hitting your child in the face while your child was driving the car? Did you stay in that relationship or leave? If you stayed, I share your embarrassment and anger."

LENGTHY WAIT FOR TRIAL

As preparations for the trial proceeded, it became clear that the process would be lengthy. In August 2012, lawyers on both sides stated they needed a year to review the evidence found in the Schenecker home. Finally, in December 2012, a trial date was set for October 7th, 2013. The trial was further delayed when Hillsborough Circuit Judge Emmett Battles granted a defense motion requesting even more time to review evidence and depose expert witnesses.

The trial eventually began on April 28th, 2014 and lasted 18 days. Julie Schenecker was found guilty of two counts of first-degree murder. She was sentenced to two concurrent life terms for the murders of her children.

Now 62 years old, Julie Schenecker serves her sentence at the Lowell Complex in Ocala, Florida. In 2023, she requested a retrial due to ineffective counsel. The judge rejected this request.

After the trial, Parker divorced Julie. Now retired, Parker remembers how his children lived and calls them his "proudest achievement in life." He continues to promote a foundation he created shortly after their deaths. The Calyx & Beau Schenecker Memorial Fund helps young people reach their goals with scholarships in the arts, humanities, and athletics.

DIFFERENT KIND OF HATE CRIME

In the city of Baguio, nestled among the mountains of Benguet, Philippines, Sef Gonzales was born in 1980. His parents, Teddy Gonzales, a lawyer, and Loiva Claridades, had been married for three years and had high hopes for their son. In 1983, their family grew with the birth of Sef's younger sister, Clodine. However, their life was upended by the devastating 1990 Luzon earthquake. Their home was destroyed, leading the family to emigrate to Sydney, Australia.

Teddy re-qualified as a lawyer and established a successful law firm specializing in immigration. By the late 1990s, the Gonzales' had established a comfortable life, purchasing a plot of land in North Ryde, where they built their home.

From the outside looking in, the Gonzales family appeared close-knit. However, beneath the surface, the devout Catholic parents were strict and held high expectations for their children, particularly Sef. They dreamed of their son excelling academically and pursuing a career in medicine or law. This vision clashed with Sef's musical aspirations. His goal was to be a famous singer.

Sef's educational journey was a struggle. After attending Parramatta Marist High School, he started the undergraduate science degree he needed to attend medical school at the University of New South Wales. However, he left after two years. He then enrolled in pre-law courses at Macquarie University. His academic performance deteriorated quickly, and he was on the brink of expulsion. In a desperate attempt to hide his failures from his parents, Sef falsified his grades. His sister Clodine discovered this deception and told their parents.

As a consequence of this fraud, Sef's parents threatened to withdraw certain privileges, including his ability to drive his prized green Ford Festiva for recreational use. Sef also had a new girlfriend, and his mother disapproved of her. Without his car, it was impossible to maintain the relationship. His girlfriend decided to break it off and return to her former boyfriend. Finally, Sef's parents threatened to disinherit him.

MURDERING THE FAMILY

On July 10th, 2001, Sef Gonzales left his father's law firm, where he worked part-time, around 4 pm, and drove home. When he walked into the house, he carried his baseball bat, which he usually kept in his car. He went and grabbed two large knives from the kitchen. He entered his sister Clodine's room, who was immersed in her studies. At first, he attempted to strangle her, but when that didn't work, he struck her head with the bat at least six times and stabbed her multiple times with a knife. Clodine died within minutes from the blunt force, head injuries, and abdominal stab wounds.

Gonzales then waited for his mother, Loiva, to arrive home around 5:30 pm. When she walked in the door, he launched an attack, inflicting multiple stab wounds and cuts to her face, neck, chest, and abdomen. In a brutal act, he cut her neck so deeply she was nearly decapitated.

The final murder occurred at 6:50 pm, when Teddy Gonzales arrived home. Sef confronted his father with one of the kitchen knives and stabbed him dozens of times. Teddy fought back but eventually succumbed to his stab wounds.

Now that his family was dead, Sef disposed of the murder weapons, his clothing, and the running shoes he had been wearing. He then staged the murders to look like a hate crime by spray painting the words "F— off Asians KKK" on a wall in the house. After showering and changing his clothes, Sef left the gruesome crime scene behind, driving to a friend's house and later to the Sydney central business district. His attempt to create an alibi for himself included a casual meal at Planet Hollywood and a visit to a video game arcade.

Later that night, after dropping his friend off, Sef returned home. At 11:48 pm, he called emergency services, feigning shock and horror at discovering his family's lifeless bodies, saying, "Please come, someone has, someone is at my parents, killed my family... they are all bleeding there on the floor."

In the aftermath of the murders, Sef acted like a bereaved son and brother. He sang the song, *One Sweet Day* by Mariah Carey at the family's funeral and gave interviews to the media, pleading for the killers to come forward. He also offered a reward of A$100,000. Yet, behind this public display of grief, Gonzales was quietly making inquiries about his inheritance, which was estimated at A$1.5 million. In addition to the family money, as a victim of crime, he was also eligible for an A$15,000 payout.

As the days passed, Gonzales moved to an apartment in Chatswood and put a deposit down on a Lexus, telling the dealership he would be using his inheritance to pay for the vehicle. Sef also traded in his parents' cars and pawned his mother's jewelry.

The NSW Police investigators initially assumed the murders were part of a robbery attempt. However, there was no forced entry and no items of value missing from the home. The medical examiner concluded that the family died over a three-hour period, and it was unlikely that thieves would remain in the house for such a long period of time. As the investigation progressed, Sef's story began to unravel.

Investigators were able to disprove Gonzales' first alibi because a neighbor claimed Sef's Ford Festiva was in the driveway during the three-hour period when the murders occurred. Sef constructed an alternate alibi, claiming he had visited a brothel at the time his family was murdered. The sex worker he claimed to be with wouldn't give him an alibi.

A search of Sef's computer showed he had researched the idea of poisoning his family, using search phrases like "methods of killing" and "poison beans" in the months prior to the murders. Through his Internet searches, he discovered poisonous beans that would kill a person in three days and leave no trace of poison. The websites Sef explored explained how to mix the beans with food to cause a slow and painful death. Sef placed orders for the beans from a US site and another in Australia. Police discovered his mother was hospitalized for food poisoning after Sef received the beans, but she recovered.

ARREST

With no alibi and other evidence mounting, Sef was charged with three counts of murder. He was denied bail and held at Silverwater Correctional Center. As the legal proceedings loomed, he was denied access to his family's estate to fund his defense.

The trial, which took place during April and May 2004, was a high-profile affair. The prosecution claimed that the murders of Teddy, 47, Loiva, 46, and Clodine, 18, were premeditated, and they explained that Sef's motive was losing his privileges and his inheritance.

On May 20th, 2004, the jury found Sef Gonzales guilty of all charges. He was sentenced to three concurrent life sentences without the possibility of parole for the murders.

THE GONZALES FAMILY HOME

Following the conclusion of the court case, the Gonzales family home built in 2000 in North Ryde, was put on the market, where it sat unsold for three years due to its notoriety.

In October 2004, a couple from Taiwan agreed to purchase the property. However, they had not been informed of the murders that took place in the house by the realtors. They discovered the tragic history of the property from a newspaper, leading to a wave of controversy. They wanted their money back.

At first, the real estate company, LJ Hooker, refused to reverse the sale, citing they had no legal obligation of disclosure. However, bad publicity led them to refund the buyers' A$80,000 deposit. The NSW Office of Fair Trading also fined the company A$21,000.

The controversy surrounding the sale led to a significant change in the NSW property law, making it illegal to fail to disclose information that could substantially impact the value of a property.

In November 2005, a year after the controversy, the house was finally sold for A$720,000, A$80,000 less than the previous price. The new buyer was fully informed of the house's history.

Sef continued to maintain his innocence and, in June 2007, was granted approval to appeal his conviction and sentence. But on November 27th, 2007, the appeal was dismissed, and his convictions remained.

DREAMS AND DESPERATION

Neil Entwistle's story began in a small town near Nottingham, England, where he was born to Clifford and Yvonne Entwistle in 1978. Raised in a working-class home, his father worked as a coal miner while his mother was a cook at a school cafeteria. His younger brother, Russell, completed the family unit. Growing up in Worksop, Neil attended the University of York, where he received a master's degree in electronic engineering.

During his university years, Neil met Rachel Souza, an American student studying abroad in York. Rachel was very outgoing and coxed for the men's rowing team. The men loved her for her American accent during the rowing events. Drawn to each other, Neil and Rachel started dating, leading to their marriage in August 2003 in Plymouth, England.

Neil said on an internet message board in the Summer of 2003, "Make bombs and other stuff for a living —

would tell you more, but I'd have to kill you. Getting married to the most amazing woman in the world this summer: Rachel. We met through rowing. Living south of the Birmingham border is my only complaint in life."

Neil eventually got a high-paying job at IBM and also did IT work for a defense technology company. At the same time, Rachel, passionate about literature and the performing arts, became a teacher of English, Drama, and Theatre Studies at St. Augustine's Catholic High School in Redditch.

The married couple moved to Worcestershire, and it was there that their daughter, Lillian, was born in 2005. Shortly after the birth of Lillian, the couple decided to move to the United States to be closer to Rachel's parents. They initially stayed with Rachel's mother and stepfather, Joseph and Priscilla Matterazzo, in Carver, Massachusetts.

FINANCIAL TROUBLES

What seemed like a promising start in a new country soon fell apart. The Entwistles struggled with finances after their move to the US because Neil had trouble finding a job in IT. He turned to the Internet to make money and set up multiple eBay accounts to sell computer products. Customers who bought from him complained to eBay that they never received their products. He started a "get rich quick" website called "Million Maker," where he helped people set up and run adult websites. He promised buyers a profit of $6000 per month, but he took their investment and later closed the website.

Neil was also looking for sex. He searched for women on Adultfriendfinder, Halfpriceescorts, Escortsnaughtynightlife, and Hotlocalescorts, creating a profile that left nothing to the imagination. "I'm looking to meet American women of all ages. I need to confirm what friends have told me that you are much better in bed than the women over the ocean, as from there. We both want the same thing, so there is little point dragging it out here."

Neil told Rachel that he had an income of $10,000 per month from an "offshore account" set up by his previous employer in the UK, but in reality, no such income or account existed. He drove a leased BMW, and he and Rachel rented a five-bedroom colonial home in Hopkinton, 26 miles west of Boston. Neil had more than $30,000 in credit card debt and had stopped making payments. Rachel asked him why their credit cards didn't work and quietly confided in her mother that she didn't understand their financial troubles because Neil had a good income from the UK.

Neil was looking for a way out and feeling the squeeze from the financial and family stress. Between his searches for jobs and escorts online, Neil started searching for "knife in neck kill" and "how to kill with a knife."

LIFE STOPS

A mere ten days after moving into their Hopkinton rental, the life of the Entwistle family took a horrifying turn.

Neil drove to his in-law's home in Carver, took a .22 caliber Colt revolver from their gun cabinet, and returned to Hopkinton. When he got home, he shot Rachel, 27, in the head and nine-month-old Lillian in the chest in the main bedroom on Friday, January 20th. He returned to Carver to return the gun before his in-laws got home from work.

On Saturday, the Entwistles had invited friends over for dinner. The friends, who were sisters named Joanne and Maureen, found the house dark and locked when they arrived at 7 pm. They called Rachel's mother, Pricilla, who also hadn't heard from the family. The police were called in to do a welfare check, and they walked through the house and found nothing out of place. One officer noticed the bed sheets and comforter in the main bedroom had been pulled off and left in a pile in the middle of the bed as if someone was getting ready to wash them. The police locked up the house and left after finding nothing amiss.

The sisters refused to leave and stayed in the driveway all night, waiting for the family to come home. The next morning, they called Rachel's mother and stepfather, who drove over to be with them at the house. The neighbors were now involved and gave the family the code to the garage so they could enter the home. Once inside, they noticed food left on plates in the dining room and quiet classical music playing. They called the police again, this time intending to file a missing persons report for the family.

When the police arrived for the second time on January 22nd, the officer noticed a faint foul odor coming from one of the bedrooms. When he moved the large pile of bedclothes in the main bedroom, he discovered the bodies of Rachel and Lillian, both in their pajamas. Rachel was lying in a fetal position and had her arm draped around Lillian. The autopsy reports would later reveal the gruesome details of their murders. Rachel died of a gunshot wound to the head, while Lillian succumbed to a gunshot wound to the torso. The bullet that had taken Lillian's life had gone through her and also pierced Rachel's left breast. The bullets were so small that the one lodged in Rachel's head remained undetected until the autopsy.

WHERE IS NEIL?

The family and the police started searching for Neil, who was quickly registered as a missing person.

Neil Entwistle had left the country. Within hours of the murders of his wife and daughter, he drove to Boston-Logan airport and purchased a one-way ticket. At approximately 5 am on January 21st, Neil boarded a British Airways flight to London. His hasty departure from the country immediately raised suspicions.

Neil rented a car and drove hundreds of miles around England before finally showing up at his parents' house in Worksop two days later. He told his parents he found his wife and daughter dead in their home and left.

A Massachusetts State Police trooper called Neil at his parents' home in Worksop. The call, which lasted two hours and was recorded, yielded a detailed account of Neil's version of the events on the morning of the murders. Neil claimed to have left his Hopkinton home around 9 am to run an errand. He claimed his wife and daughter were alive and well in the couple's main bedroom. When he returned home around 11 am he found them both shot dead. He covered their bodies with a blanket but didn't alert the authorities. Distraught, he told police he attempted suicide with a knife but was unable to do so. He then drove to the Matterazzos' house to kill himself with a .22 caliber revolver. Finding the house locked, he decided to fly home to England to see his parents.

"I pulled the covers over them and the only thing I could think of was the knives we had got downstairs. I pulled the big one out and held it towards my chest. I think it was just the thought of how much it was going to hurt. I just couldn't do it. I don't know why I didn't [call the emergency services]."

FROM THE RECORDED PHONE
CONVERSATION WITH NEIL
ENTWISTLE AND MASSACHUSETTS
STATE TROOPER ROBERT
MANNING

Two police officers from the US flew to London to speak with Neil and had set up a meeting with him at the US Embassy. Neil agreed to meet them initially, but his attorney advised him to cancel the meeting.

In Massachusetts, Rachel and Lillian were buried in the same casket at Evergreen Cemetery in Kingston, Massachusetts, and hundreds of mourners attended the funeral. Neil didn't fly in for the funeral. He was not mentioned at the service, and his name did not appear on the headstone, which reflected Rachel's maiden name of Souza. He did, however, send flowers. One orange rose surrounded by white lilies, with the message, "My Orange Rose and my Lilly for always. XOXOXOX."

After the funerals, Lillian's birth and death certificates were edited to read "father unknown."

THE INVESTIGATION CONTINUES

The ongoing investigation revealed that Neil's DNA was found on the handle of the same .22 handgun his father-in-law, Joseph Matterazzo owned. Neil claimed in his telephone interview that he had only used the gun once, months earlier, while practicing at Matterazzo's shooting club. DNA matching that of his wife, Rachel, was discovered on the gun's muzzle, and a set of keys to the Matterazzo's house were found in the car Neil had left at Boston's Logan International Airport. He had the means to let himself in the house, contradicting his recorded testimony that said his in-law's house was locked and he couldn't get in.

Given the evidence and his unconvincing narrative, Neil quickly became a suspect in the investigation, and the Middlesex County District Attorney's Office issued an international arrest warrant.

In the UK, Neil was moving on with his life. Even as the media swarmed his Worksop residence in early February, he dined with his old rowing buddies from York University in Notting Hill and went to the cinema.

LONDON ARREST

Neil knew the police were looking for him, and he got on the London tube at Ladbroke Grove. He was apprehended at the Royal Oak subway station by the

Metropolitan Police. Found on him was a blue bag holding a journal that detailed his plans to auction off his story to the most generous offer.

In the journal, he declared his love for his "Orange Rose" and "my Lilly," and he referred to his wife as his "soul-mate" and "dearest companion."

The journal also had drafts of letters addressed to book editors. In one letter, he identified himself as a trusted ally of "Neil Entwistle" who wanted to share his perspective on the tragedy. The letter posed a question: "How much are you willing to offer for exclusive access to the complete tale?"

Although the extradition to the US could have taken months, by February 15th, Neil was on his way back to the US, having chosen not to challenge the extradition proceedings. Upon his arrival, he was arraigned at Framingham District Court and ordered to be held without bail at Middlesex County Jail in Cambridge.

Neil was charged with two counts of murder, illegal possession of a firearm and illegal possession of ammunition. He pleaded not guilty to all charges.

While awaiting trial, officers at the Middlesex County jail discovered letters from Neil to his parents and his legal team. The letters indicated he was deeply depressed and might be contemplating suicide. For his safety, Neil was transferred to Bridgewater State Hospital for mental evaluation before being returned to Middlesex County.

As the legal proceedings against Neil progressed, concerns arose about the high-profile nature of the case and whether it would be possible for him to receive a fair trial. Some media reports suggested that potential jurors had already decided his guilt. After numerous delays, the Middlesex Superior Court finally started the juror selection process.

The trial was marked by a series of legal battles. Neil's legal team fought vigorously against the prosecution's proposals to use DNA evidence. They also tried to suppress other evidence found in the family home due to the lack of a warrant during its seizure. The defense proposed an alternate narrative. They suggested that Rachel killed the baby and then killed herself. Neil's defense team called no witnesses, and Entwistle himself did not testify in his own defense.

The prosecution's case, built on the compelling DNA evidence from the murder weapon and the chilling details of the crime, proved to be too overwhelming. Neil cried in the courtroom as the jury was shown video footage of the house, the crime scene, and the bodies. Lillian's bloodstained pajamas were also shown in the courtroom, with a bullet hole clearly visible through the small garment.

VERDICT

The jury found Entwistle guilty of all charges.

The sentence handed down by Judge Diane Kottmyer was two life sentences without the possibility of parole. In addition to the life sentences, Kottmyer imposed ten years of probation on the firearms and ammunition charges to run concurrently. The court also stipulated that Neil could never profit from the sale of his story.

ENTWISTLE'S PARENTS

Meanwhile, on the other side of the Atlantic, Neil's parents filed a complaint of harassment with the UK Press Complaints Commission against their local newspaper, the *Worksop Guardian*, in October 2008. The complaint was ultimately rejected. Despite the overwhelming evidence against their son, Neil's parents continued to assert his innocence. They believed that Rachel was the true killer and that Neil would eventually be cleared and released from prison. In a heartbreaking testament to a mother's love, Neil's mother stated after the trial, "We are devastated to learn that the evidence points to Rachel murdering our grandchild and then committing suicide. I knew Rachel was depressed. Our son will now go to jail for loving, honoring, and protecting his wife's memory."

As the legal battles waged on, Neil began serving his

sentence at the Souza-Baranowski Correctional Center. However, due to threats on his life, he was placed in protective custody and later transferred to Old Colony Correctional Center, a medium-security prison in Bridgewater, Massachusetts.

The Department of Corrections confirmed that the threats against Entwistle's life were serious. Neil had shaved his head down to the scalp in an attempt to join a white supremacist prison group that said they would protect him. The group's leader told him that as a child-killer his life was still in danger. One prison official said he overheard a member of the white supremacist gang saying, "It's a nice gesture, on your part, but we're still going to kill you."

THE CHILDREN

Johanna Maria Magdalena Ritschel, known later in life as Magda Goebbels, was born out of wedlock in Berlin in 1901 to Auguste Behrend and Oskar Ritschel. Her parents married later that year but divorced when Magda was still young. In 1908, her mother married Richard Friedländer, a wealthy Jewish merchant from Brussels. He adopted Magda and gave the young girl his surname.

During her childhood, Magda became friends with Lisa Arlosoroff, and as a young teen, she developed a friendship and intimate relationship with Lisa's brother, Haim. Magda wore a Star of David necklace gifted by Haim for a brief period and accompanied him to Jewish youth club meetings. However, their off-and-on relationship did not last beyond the early 1920s, though they remained in contact even after Haim immigrated to the Middle East.

Magda and her adopted family remained in Brussels until 1914. When the Germans invaded Belgium during WWI, the family returned to Berlin. In 1919, after divorcing Friedländer, Magda's mother enrolled her in a boarding school, the prestigious Ladies' College Holzhausen in Goslar, Germany.

In 1920, while returning to boarding school on a train, Magda met Günther Quandt, a wealthy German businessman twice her age. Quandt began courting her and giving Magda gifts. He insisted that she change her surname back to her maiden name, Ritschel since she had borne the Jewish name Friedländer for many years after her adoption. On January 4th, 1921, a 19-year-old Magda married the 37-year-old Quandt, and their first child Harald was born that November.

Magda soon grew frustrated in her marriage. Quandt spent little time with her and focused more on expanding his business empire across Germany. Together, they took care of six children, including Harald, two sons from Quandt's previous marriage, and three children of a deceased friend the couple had adopted. By 1929, their relationship was falling apart. Quandt discovered Magda was having an affair, leading to their separation and divorce by the end of that year. Despite the affair, Magda's divorce settlement was quite generous. Magda was now a wealthy, 29-year-old woman searching for something more.

THE NAZI PARTY

In 1930, Magda attended a meeting of the Nazi Party where she was impressed by one of the speakers, Joseph Goebbels. She joined the party on September 1st, 1930, and began volunteering, though she was not seen as politically active. Magda moved from the local party branch to the headquarters in Berlin and was asked to assist Goebbels, who was now Hitler's propaganda minister.

Magda and Goebbels became romantically involved during a short trip to Weimar in February 1931. By April, they began making plans for their future together. Goebbels wrote in his diary, "We have made a solemn vow to each other: When we have conquered the Reich, we will become man and wife. I am very happy." Their relationship progressed quickly, with Magda's flat becoming a favorite meeting place for Hitler and other Nazi officials.

Eager to advance their wedding date, Magda and Goebbels were married on December 19th, 1931, with Hitler serving as a witness. They went on to have six children - Helga, Hilde, Helmut, Holde, Hedda, and Heide born between 1932 and 1940. All of their names started with "H" to honor Adolf Hitler. However, Goebbels had numerous affairs during their marriage, and Magda wanted a divorce. In the Summer of 1938, the union faced its end due to another romance between Goebbels and the Czech actress Lida Varlova. To avoid a scandal, Hitler stepped in, insisting that Goebbels end the affair.

Magda developed a close personal relationship with Hitler through her marriage to Goebbels and was one of the Führer's most trusted confidants. She would act as an unofficial representative of the regime and could enjoy the lavish lifestyle that accompanied her prominence in the Nazi Party.

When war broke out in 1939, Magda lived up to the image of a patriotic German mother. Her eldest son from her first marriage, Harald Quandt, became a Luftwaffe pilot fighting at the front. He was fond of his mother's new husband, Joseph Goebbels, and wanted to participate in the war effort. Magda herself trained as a Red Cross nurse and worked for the electronics company Telefunken, commuting alongside colleagues on the bus each day. She also helped entertain the wives of foreign heads of state and comforted war widows.

Joseph and Magda Goebbels remained outwardly loyal to Hitler, publicly supporting him and the Nazi regime. But privately, Magda began to have doubts, especially as the war dragged on and German defeat looked likely. On November 9th, 1942, during a gathering listening to one of Hitler's speeches, she turned off the radio, saying, "My God, what a lot of rubbish." By 1944, she was reported to have said that Hitler no longer listened to reason and only believed those telling him what he wanted to hear.

Magda was treated for depression and was frequently hospitalized for weeks. She also suffered from trigeminal neuralgia, an intense nerve pain in her face that often left her bedridden. Her poor health continued even as the Soviet Red Army approached Berlin in the war's final days. But despite her private doubts and ailments, Magda would remain a supporter of Hitler right to the end.

In late April 1945, with Berlin surrounded by the advancing Soviet forces, Magda and Joseph Goebbels moved into the Führerbunker connected to Hitler's lower bunker under the Chancellery garden. On April 30th, Magda was among the last to see Hitler and Eva Braun before their suicides.

THE CHILDREN

After Hitler's death, witnesses state Magda refused offers to smuggle the children out of Berlin, insisting they must stay by their father's side. She told Hitler's secretary, Traudl Junge, that she felt the children would have no place in the world after National Socialism and that death was better than the shame they would have endured.

On May 1st, Magda and Joseph Goebbels asked SS dentist Helmut Kunz to inject morphine into their six children to render them unconscious. This initial step needed to happen so the children could be poisoned with cyanide. Kunz initially refused but was later told it was not a request but a direct order. Magda went into the room where the children were sleeping and told them not to be afraid. She said the doctor would give them an injection that all children and soldiers get. The Goebbels children, whose ages ranged between 12 and four years old, were left to the dentist to receive their injections. It took Kunz 10 minutes to inject all the children with morphine. Different accounts exist of who administrated the cyanide itself, with some blaming it on Hitler's physician, Dr. Ludwig Stumpfegger, but Magda was the orchestrator of the deaths of her children.

After the children were dead, Magda and Joseph Goebbels ascended the stairs from the bunker and entered the Chancellery garden. There are differing accounts of their suicide method, but most agree they took cyanide ampules and were shot afterward to ensure their deaths. Their bodies were discovered the next day by Soviet troops, burned but still recognizable.

In the following years, the remains of Goebbels' family were repeatedly exhumed and reburied by the Soviets until 1970, when they were definitively cremated and scattered to prevent the site from becoming a neo-Nazi shrine.

Harald Quandt was the only one of Magda's children to survive World War II. He became a successful West German businessman in the 1950s and 1960s. He was killed in a private plane crash over Italy in 1967 at the age of 46.

FATE

This harrowing tale began in the mid-1990s when 20-year-old Steven Pladl encountered 15-year-old Alyssa in an Internet chatroom. The online encounter soon evolved into a physical relationship when Steven traveled to San Antonio, Texas, to meet Alyssa. She was entranced by Steven and ran away from her home and her family to live with him in New York.

Alyssa became pregnant at 16 and gave birth to their first child, a girl they named Denise Pladl. Alyssa claimed that Steven didn't bond with Denise and never took care of her. According to Alyssa, Steven subjected their infant daughter to a horrifying regimen of abuse, inflicting physical pain that left the child "black and blue." He even attempted to drown her. Steven would scream at Denise when she cried. Eventually, he said he couldn't stand the screaming and crying anymore, so he placed her in an ice chest. Sometimes, he would put a blanket in there to keep a crack open, but other times, he would shut the lid and not allow Alyssa to open it for a few minutes. When she did open it, she claimed the baby would be gasping for air and sweating.

Faced with such a dire situation, Alyssa decided to put eight-month-old Denise up for adoption. She believed that while living under the same roof as Steven, her daughter would not have a chance at a regular or healthy life. In making this decision, Alyssa hoped to provide Denise with an opportunity for a better future. After Denise was adopted, Alyssa stayed with Steven, married him, and had two more children with him.

DENISE BECOMES KATIE

Denise Pladl's life took a hopeful turn when she was adopted by Anthony and Kelly Fusco, who renamed her Katie Rose Fusco. For a while, it seemed that Katie had escaped the cruel past that had defined her first year of life. However, this respite proved to be temporary.

EIGHTEEN YEARS LATER

In August of 2016, an 18-year-old Katie, driven by a desire to understand her roots, reached out to her biological parents, Steven and Alyssa Pladl, via Facebook. They met in Knightdale, North Carolina, where the Pladls were living, and after some deliberation, Katie decided to move in with them and their other two children. This decision was met with apprehension by her adoptive parents, yet they supported her, likely under-standing her need to connect with her biological family as an adult.

By the time Katie moved in, Steven and Alyssa's relation-ship had deteriorated to the point of separation, and they were living in the same house but sleeping in sepa-rate bedrooms. In the following months, Katie and Steven developed a close relationship that seemed to transcend the typical father-daughter bond. One day, when Alyssa confronted them about this, Steven claimed it was none of her business and stormed out of the house with Katie. Alyssa subsequently moved out in November 2016, and the custody of the other two children was shared between her and Steven.

In May 2017, the disturbing reality of Steven and Katie's peculiar closeness was revealed. Alyssa stumbled upon a passage written in one of their children's journals, revealing that Steven and Katie were engaged in an incestuous sexual relationship. Not only was Katie preg-nant, but the other children had been told that Katie was now their stepmother. The shocking revelation led Alyssa to confront Steven, who confirmed the situation, leaving Alyssa no choice but to report the situation to the police.

TABOO RELATIONSHIP

Steven and Katie, seemingly oblivious to societal norms

and laws, continued to deepen their illicit relationship. On July 20th, 2017, they married in Parkton, Maryland, falsifying their marriage documents to hide their biological relationship. Their wedding was attended by Steven's mother and Katie's adoptive parents, Anthony and Kelly Fusco.

In September 2017, Katie gave birth to their child, Bennett Kieron Pladl. Their life was disrupted in January 2018 when the couple was arrested on charges of incest, adultery, and contributing to delinquency. Steven's attorney defended his client by arguing that the relationship was consensual and that Steven was so deeply in love with Katie that it "outweighed the issue of them being biologically related." He cited Steven's previous marital problems as a contributing factor.

Following the arrest, the court ordered Steven and Katie to have no contact with each other. At the same time, the custody of their infant son, Bennett, was temporarily given to Steven's mother, but there were no restrictions keeping Steven from seeing the baby. Katie's bond required her to return to her adoptive parents' home. This decision marked a significant turning point in her life as she attempted to distance herself from the relationship. She called Steven and told him it was over — she didn't want to be married anymore.

Stephen called his mother and said he was on his way to her place to pick up Bennett, and he told her that he and Bennett were going to drive to New York to see Katie and then he was going to leave Bennett with Katie, but that's not what Stephen did. On April 11th, Steven brought the baby back to his house and murdered him. It is unclear how the baby died, but it is assumed he was shot.

Then Steven drove through the night over 600 miles from North Carolina to New York, where the Fuscos lived. When he arrived, he parked his car across the street from the Fusco house and waited until Katie and her adoptive dad, Anthony, left the house. On Thursday, April 12th, Steven followed them in the truck and pulled up alongside it when it stopped at a stop sign. Steven opened fire with an AR-15-style weapon and killed Katie and Anthony Fusco.

Steven Pall drove about five minutes away from the scene of the murders and called his mother, telling her what he had done with Bennet and about the other shooting. Steven's mother called 911, and first responders found the boy's body stuffed into a closet in Steven's house. After the phone call, Steven Pladl shot and killed himself.

Katie, Anthony Fusco, and Bennett were buried together in Saint Charles Cemetery, Dover Plains, New York.

544 CASTLE DRIVE

Jeffrey MacDonald's early life was the picture of small-town achievement on the path to the American dream. Born in 1943 in Jamaica, Queens, and raised in nearby Patchogue on Long Island, MacDonald was voted "most popular" and "most likely to succeed" in high school. He served as student council president and was named king of the senior prom. Bright and driven, MacDonald won a scholarship to Princeton University in 1962 to study biology and psychology on a pre-med track.

It was at Patchogue High that MacDonald first met Colette Stevenson, who would later become his wife. MacDonald recalled noticing the shy girl in the school hallway as a freshman and soon asked her out to the movies. Though they dated briefly, the young romance faded over the summer, and Colette told him the relationship was over. McDonald started dating another young woman named Penny Wells, but that didn't last long, and MacDonald and Colette reconnected when he was at Princeton. McDonald was casually dating several women when Colette told him she was pregnant in 1963 at age 18. They decided to get married, and their first child, Kimberley, was born in April 1964.

After Princeton, MacDonald attended Northwestern University Medical School in Chicago on a scholarship. He juggled his intensive studies with jobs to support his young family, which grew again with the birth of his daughter Kristen in 1967. After graduating from medical school in 1968, MacDonald completed an internship in New York City before being commissioned into the Army in June 1969. That August, Captain MacDonald, Colette, and their two little girls embarked on their new military life at Fort Bragg in Fayetteville, North Carolina, where MacDonald served as a Green Beret medical officer.

In late 1969, just before Christmas and with his wife about three months into her pregnancy with their third child and first son, MacDonald secretly purchased a Shetland pony for his daughters. He and his father-in-law took the family to see the pony on Christmas Day. The girls decided to call it "Trooper." That same month, Colette wrote a letter to college friends, expressing her happiness and the normality of her life. She mentioned that the arrival of their son next summer would make her family complete. Outwardly, all signs pointed to continued success for the handsome young doctor with the beautiful family. But this would be their last Christmas together as a family.

In the pre-dawn hours of February 17th, 1970, a chilling call awoke the Fort Bragg military police switchboard. "Help... stabbing... five forty-four Castle Drive!" The incoherent plea came from the on-base home of Captain Jeffrey MacDonald. Responding military police officers arrived at the darkened house and circled to the back door, which was left open and unlocked. Stepping inside, the officers came upon a horrifying scene.

On the floor of the main bedroom lay Colette MacDonald, 26 years old and pregnant with her third child. Her partially nude body, covered with blood, was on the floor. She had been bludgeoned and stabbed multiple times. Both of her arms appeared broken, likely from attempts to shield her face. Nearby, the word "PIG" was scrawled in blood on the headboard. Five-year-old Kimberley was found dead in her bedroom, with head wounds and multiple stab wounds. Two-year-old Kristen had been stabbed several times as she lay on her bed, clutching a bottle, surrounded by stuffed animals.

Jeffrey MacDonald himself was discovered collapsed near his wife's corpse, alive but wounded, his breathing labored from a collapsed lung. When officers tried to speak to him, he moaned, "My wife and kids are dead!" He spoke of hearing his daughters' screams as intruders attacked them. MacDonald claimed that four hippie-like assailants—three men and a blond woman—had broken in and chanted "Acid is groovy" and "Kill the pigs" as they attacked him with a club and ice pick before turning on his sleeping family. He yelled at the officers,

"Jesus Christ! Look at my wife! I'm gonna kill those goddamned acid heads!"

THE INVESTIGATION BEGINS

In the hours after the murders, the military police inspected the occupants of every vehicle on and near Fort Bragg. Based on MacDonald's description of the four assailants, they were looking for two white males, one black male, and a blond white female wearing a floppy hat. Despite intensive efforts, the military police could not find them, and the search was called off by 6 am.

The investigators found the weapons believed to be used in the murder just outside the residence's rear entrance. They found an Old Hickory kitchen knife, an ice pick, and a 31-inch piece of bloodstained lumber. The items had been wiped down and were devoid of any fingerprints.

At the hospital, MacDonald's minor wounds were in stark contrast to those inflicted upon his wife and daughters. According to police and medical records, he had a concussion, a small knife wound between two ribs, and scratches on his face.

The MacDonalds' neighbors were interviewed, and none of them had heard strange noises in the early morning hours. However, they did recall hearing Colette's voice raised in anger earlier the previous evening. The neighboring family's 16-year-old daughter, who sometimes babysat for the MacDonalds, shared with investigators that the couple seemed more distant and communicated less around her.

SUSPICIONS

Soon after the murders, Jeffrey MacDonald was considered a suspect. Army investigators doubted his story about the "hippie group" breaking in. They found no evidence of any intruders. Forensic analysis added to investigators' skepticism. A large amount of Kimberley's blood was found in the main bedroom, though her body lay in her own room, and MacDonald's blood and Colette's blood were found on Kristen's mattress. MacDonald had explicitly said in a police interview that he hadn't moved any bodies, and he was attacked first before his wife and daughters were murdered.

In April 1970, Army investigators interviewed MacDonald, confronting him with the inconsistencies and evidence that troubled them. They asked him to take a polygraph test, which he initially agreed to but then declined. The following month, the Army formally charged MacDonald with the murders.

In August, a courier named William Posey said he knew the mysterious blond woman that MacDonald was referring to. She was Helena Stoeckley, a local 17-year-old drug addict who was also a police informant. When questioned by police about the murders, Stoeckley admitted that she was out for a drive that night with some male friends, but she couldn't recall all her actions that night because she was high on mescaline. The police didn't detain her.

～

MacDonald attended a preliminary hearing a few months later, and things went in his favor. While investigators had found no physical evidence of intruders in the MacDonald's home, a military police officer and first responder on the scene testified that he saw a woman with blond hair and a hat about one block from the house before they arrived. He said he remembered this because of the late hour and the rainy weather. MacDonald's attorney claimed that the investigative team had made several mistakes by "trampling all over" the crime scene. The Army dismissed the charges due to insufficient evidence that October and MacDonald was released.

After the murder charges were dropped, MacDonald did several media interviews. He wrote letters to multiple magazines and newspapers, expressing his readiness to find the real killers. He often exaggerated the circumstances of the murders, including the severity of his wounds, saying he had 23 injuries, some of which were life-threatening.

MacDonald was honorably discharged from the military, and the case might have ended there, but Alfred Kassab, MacDonald's father-in-law, became suspicious after watching the media interviews. Once a vocal supporter, Kassab started to believe his son-in-law was lying. After his investigation, he discovered that before the murders, MacDonald was having an affair with his former girlfriend, Penny Wells. MacDonald also started dating another woman who worked on the Army base three weeks after the murders.

GRAND JURY

Kassab pushed the Justice Department to reopen the case, and it took several years for them to rule the case worthy of a hearing and grand jury. On August 12th, 1974, U.S. District Judge Franklin Dupree in Raleigh, North Carolina, presided over a grand jury that called 75 witnesses for testimony. The initial testimony was given by MacDonald, which spanned over five days. MacDonald justified the multiple false statements he had given to the Kassabs and various media outlets over the years, explaining that he didn't actually pursue the real killers and that these statements were meant to appease his in-laws. He claimed to have suffered more stab and puncture wounds than were documented in his medical records, attributing this discrepancy to medical negligence. When asked by the prosecutor if he would agree to a polygraph or sodium amytal test to confirm his narrative, MacDonald refused.

The list of witnesses also included surgeons from the hospital who had examined MacDonald after the murders. They testified that MacDonald was not in serious medical peril apart from a punctured lung. Aside from a minor stab wound on his upper left arm and stomach, they confirmed that MacDonald had no other stab wounds.

Former psychiatry chief Bruce Bailey, who had previously testified at MacDonald's military hearing in 1970, took the stand. Bailey testified that MacDonald would intermittently become emotional and tearful when discussing his family and the circumstances of their deaths but would recover quickly. Bailey found MacDonald to be a dominant figure concerned about how people perceived him. He said MacDonald often resorted to verbal outbursts to express his intense emotions. Although Bailey did not diagnose MacDonald with a mental disorder, he couldn't rule out the possibility of MacDonald committing family homicide under severe stress. This testimony was followed by a psychologist based in Philadelphia who agreed that if MacDonald had indeed committed such a violent act, he could successfully repress the memory of the incident.

MacDonald was again asked to take the witness stand and answer questions about his infidelity and the contradictions between his statement of the events and the physical evidence. MacDonald got angry and yelled, "I have no idea! I don't even know what crap you're trying to feed me!"

The grand jury indicted MacDonald on three counts of murder, and he was arrested, pleaded not guilty, and was released on a $100,000 bond.

IN AND OUT OF PRISON

MacDonald was free for the four years it took for the trial to begin. It didn't go well for him, and after a dramatic three-week trial, the jury convicted MacDonald of second-degree murder for his wife Colette and elder daughter Kimberley and first-degree murder for his daughter Kristen. He was sentenced to three consecutive life terms.

In 1980, the Fourth Circuit Court of Appeals overturned his conviction due to the lengthy delay in bringing him to trial, and MacDonald was released for two years. But the ruling was itself reversed in 1982 by the Supreme Court, and MacDonald was returned to prison.

MacDonald filed numerous appeals over the following decades, citing issues ranging from suppressed evidence to prosecutor misconduct. DNA testing in 2006 did not exonerate him, and courts repeatedly upheld his conviction.

MacDonald's defenders have seized on unidentified fingerprints and fibers found at the crime scene to prove his innocence claim. They also point to unsourced black wool fibers found on Colette's body and other evidence they argue was suppressed by prosecutors. But prosecutors have dismissed these as inconclusive anomalies that would not have affected the jury's verdict.

Media interest in the MacDonald case surged with the 1983 bestselling book *Fatal Vision* by Joe McGinniss, which concluded MacDonald was guilty and a psychopath. MacDonald sued McGinniss over the book, and they settled out of court in 1987, but MacDonald received only a fraction of the settlement due to his in-laws' legal efforts.

MacDonald, now 77, asked the U.S. District Court to release him under a federal compassionate release law due to his age, kidney disease, skin cancer, and high blood pressure. U.S. District Judge Terrence Boyle held a hearing on MacDonald's request in March, and in April 2021, he rejected it.

DEPTHS OF DESPAIR

Francis "Frank" Stack was a Korean War veteran who had served in the Marine Corps. After his military service, he worked as a lineman for Commonwealth Edison and was a longtime resident of Elmhurst, Illinois. The 82-year-old Frank was described as a pillar of his community — the kind of neighbor who was the first to welcome new families and always willing to lend a hand. He regularly brought baked goods from the farmer's market to share with his neighbors. Frank could be stubborn and quick-tempered at times, but many who knew him also saw him as charming. His wife Joan was his opposite — quiet, deeply Catholic, and focused on taking impeccable care of their home and family.

Together, Frank and Joan had four children. Their daughters Barbara and Gloria were married and had children of their own. Frank Jr., known as "Frankie" and Mary, had developmental disabilities. Frankie, age 48, lived in a group home and was nonverbal, with a very low IQ. Mary, age 57, also lived in a group home and had profound intellectual disabilities. Frank and Joan, also 82, had raised Frankie and Mary at home until the late 1990s. At some point, it became too difficult for the aging parents to care for their adult children. The Stacks worked diligently through Medicaid, Medicare, private insurance, and other programs to find and fund group homes where Frankie and Mary could live safely and comfortably despite their special needs. It was emotionally challenging for Frank and Joan to visit their adult children in the residential facilities. Still, after decades of caring for their son and daughter, they knew it needed to be done.

Frank harbored guilt over his children's disabilities and had mentioned to family members on more than one occasion that he believed they might have been caused by something he was exposed to during his military service. He carried this pain quietly throughout his life as he and Joan raised and cared for their disabled children.

Frank's health declined from severe sciatica as he grew older, and he had trouble getting around. But he remained devoted to his family, particularly his son Frankie. Frank saw Frankie at least once a week at his residential home, and he took him on drives and brought him home for dinner so Joan could see him. Frank was very protective of his son and made sure the staff at Frankie's group home took care of any issues.

LABOR DAY WEEKEND

On Labor Day weekend in 2014, Frank Stack went to the group home where his 48-year-old son Frankie lived and told the supervisor on duty that Frankie's mother, Joan, wanted to see her son for the holiday. This was not unusual because Frank regularly took Frankie home for visits. He then went to the group home where his 57-year-old daughter Mary resided and told the staff there that Joan was very ill and wanted Mary to come home for a visit. These claims weren't true, but the staff had no reason to suspect Frank was lying.

Frank brought Frankie and Mary back to the small bungalow home where they grew up. Joan, who was bedridden, was under the care of hospice workers for severe arthritis. That evening, after the hospice aides had left for the day, Frank called the group home supervisor who cared for Frankie. He confessed he had shot and killed Joan, Frankie, and Mary. The supervisor pleaded desperately for Frank not to harm himself or anyone else. But when police arrived at the house, they found Frank had shot himself after tidying up the scene and carefully laying out important documents. Joan and Mary died instantly from their wounds, while Frankie sustained fatal injuries but may not have died immediately. The DuPage County Coroner confirmed that Frank Stack shot his wife and children and then shot himself.

The residents of Frankie's and Mary's group homes were devastated when they learned of the tragedy. Frankie's housemates, in particular, took the news very hard. One nonverbal man who lived with Frankie immediately began sobbing when told what had happened, heartbreakingly aware of the loss of his friend.

At Mary's residence, when one of her housemates found out Mary had been killed, the first thing she did was scream and point to a portrait of Mary's parents on the wall, pleading for it to be taken down in her grief and confusion.

The surviving daughters, Gloria and Barbara, declined to speak publicly about the details. But on the night of the murders, Gloria told police her father had been a saint his whole life for caring for her disabled siblings. In a later statement, she referred to her parents as "truly amazing people."

Some in the community saw Frank as brave, seemingly sparing his family further suffering. However, experts resoundingly condemned the mercy killings as unjustifiable and criminal, regardless of the circumstances.

OBSESSION

Grant Amato was born in 1989 in the small town of Chuluota, Florida. He was the son of Chad and Margaret Amato, a pharmacist, and a senior operations manager, respectively. As a child, Grant grew up with his brother Cody, and they had an older half-brother, Jason, who lived nearby.

The Amato brothers' childhood was marked by shared experiences. They attended Timber Creek High School together, and their interest in health led them to join the weightlifting team. Their academic paths also mirrored each other for a time. Grant and Cody chose to study at the University of Central Florida, where they pursued nursing. Their shared ambition led them to further their studies, with both brothers studying to become nurse anesthetists.

FAMILY PLANS

The brothers had agreed to buy their parent's house in Chuluota when they were financially able to do so that their parents could retire in Tennessee. Plans changed when Cody successfully graduated from the nurse anesthetist program, while Grant chose to drop out. Despite this setback, Grant found employment at AdventHealth Orlando as a nurse, seemingly setting himself on a stable career path.

In June 2018, Grant was arrested and fired from his job amid allegations of stealing and improperly administering medication to patients. Hospital staff had discovered eight empty vials of the sedative propofol, which hadn't been ordered by any doctor, sitting in patient rooms assigned to Grant. The charges were later dropped, but Grant had lost his job for good and had difficulty finding another nursing position.

In the wake of his professional downfall, Grant found himself adrift. He spent most of his time watching pornography and video game streaming on Twitch. Grant explained to his family that he could make a full-time income just from streaming. His family knew he was going through a rough period and willingly paid for the equipment and streaming setup.

Instead of game streaming, Grant's actual online activities were spent on adult websites like MyFreeCams.

There, Grant stumbled upon Silviya Ventsislavova, a Bulgarian cam model who went by the alias "Silvie" online. Grant was infatuated with Silvie and spent up to four hours each night paying for her virtual company.

Under the guise of being a successful video gamer, he lavished her with gifts, including lingerie and sex toys, while also paying an excessive amount for her time. All this was financed by taking money from his family under the pretense of developing his Twitch career. Grant even stole his brother Cody's guns and sold them for cash to give to Silvie so he could continue to watch her online. In a short period, Grant had squandered $200,000 of his family's money on his obsession with the cam girl.

Chad had been forced to refinance his home to settle $150,000 of Grant's outstanding debts. The father and son argued daily, and Chad asked Grant to leave the house. He went to stay with his aunt, Donna Amato. During Grant's stay, Donna discovered unexplained transactions in her bank account. After quickly investigating the charges, Donna determined that Grant initiated them. Both Chad and Margaret Amato begged Donna not to take legal action, and they offered to reimburse the total amount taken by Grant.

The family staged an intervention and sent Grant to a rehabilitation facility for porn and internet addiction. The rehabilitation, which cost them $15,000, was seen as a final effort to save Grant from his self-destructive path, but Grant left partway through the program. The Amato family had contacted Sylvie while Grant was in rehab, and she blocked Grant's account.

When he returned home, his father, Chad, gave him some new guidelines. He had to find a job, and he was prohibited from any contact with Silvie.

Grant had no interest in this and tried to contact Sylvie immediately. Finding out he was blocked, he wrote a note to one of his online cam girl groups apologizing for his behavior.

"Everyone, I ask for your forgiveness regarding my stupidity. I will never be able to forgive myself for making Silvie sad and for betraying her trust in me. Despite the many things that I have tried to currently emphasize to her...I care for her deeply and wish for an actual second chance with her and the room.

"I think it is safe to say by now that everyone here knows that I made a drastic mistake with Silvie. I upset her, made her very sad, and ruined the end of December and beginning of January for her. I won't go into great detail because that is not the purpose of this message, but I lied to her and you guys from the beginning about myself. I am not a professional gamer, did not own my own house, and did not drive a BMW. The major one here was the gamer."

The pull of his obsession with Sylvie was too strong. Grant manipulated his mother into letting him use her phone to contact Silvie. When Chad discovered this, he ordered Grant to leave their home for good. This decision would lead to a chain of events ending the Amato family forever.

THE MURDERS

On January 24th, 2019, Grant was supposed to be packing his clothing to leave the house. He waited until his mother was engrossed in her computer, and he approached her from behind and shot her in the back of the head with an IWI Jericho 941 pistol, instantly killing her.

He then waited for his father, Chad, to come home. As Chad stepped into the kitchen, Grant aimed and fired twice, leaving his father dead on the floor. The deadly sequence of events didn't end there. Grant used their father's phone to send an urgent text message to lure his brother, Cody, home during his nursing shift.

Cody took the bait, and Grant shot him when he walked in the door, leaving his body curled up in a fetal position on the floor. Once the murders were complete, Grant attempted to stage the crime scene as a murder-suicide. He placed the murder weapon next to Cody's body, hoping to pin the blame on his deceased brother.

When Cody failed to show up for work the following day, his concerned coworkers alerted the police, prompting them to perform a wellness check at the Amato residence. Arriving at the scene at 9 am, they noticed three cars parked at the house on Sultan Circle. Despite repeated knocks, no one responded from inside the house. This led deputies to break in after they couldn't unlock the back door. Upon entering, they discovered three lifeless bodies: Chad on his back on the kitchen floor, Cody still in his hospital scrubs in a storage room, and Margaret sprawled over the desk in their home office.

The search for Grant Amato started when they found his white Honda Accord missing from the house. The vehicle was later located at a hotel in Orange County where Grant had checked in. He was taken in for "investigative detention" but released as the sheriff's office continued their probe. Several days later, the police returned to the hotel and arrested Grant. He claimed he knew nothing about the murders, and when pictures of his dead brother and his parents were shown to him, he teared up but wouldn't confess. The police brought in his half-brother Jason to speak with him, but he refused to talk. The police charged him with three counts of murder.

The trial of Grant Amato began on July 15th, 2019, and

it started with the prosecutor announcing their intention to seek the death penalty. The prosecution's crime scene analysts were among the first to testify, and Grant's half-brother, Jason, also testified against him.

However, the jurors were not unanimous in their guilty verdict, and the death penalty could not be imposed without unanimity. Grant was sentenced to three life terms without the possibility of parole.

When asked if he felt any remorse, Grant, still not taking responsibility, said, "My family has been blaming me for months for ruining their lives, stealing, and not following the rules of the home, so I might as well be blamed for this too."

ALIAS

Frederick Deeming, born in Kent, England, in 1853, started his childhood with the label "difficult child." Deeming's father, Thomas, suffered from bouts of mental illness, including hearing voices and seeing ghosts. He also regularly beat his son. After the death of his mother, Frederick Deeming ran away at age 16 to go to sea. Over the next two decades, he became adept at fraud, thievery, bigamy, and murder.

By the time he was 30 years old, he had made his way to Australia, living primarily in Sydney and Melbourne, working odd jobs while also continuing his criminal activities. He worked as a gasfitter but was caught stealing brass fittings from his employer and sentenced to six weeks in prison. After being released, he continued working in Sydney but was arrested again for fraud and sent to jail.

During his years in Australia, Deeming married his first wife, Marie James, and they had two Australian-born daughters. After multiple arrests, Deeming left the continent, taking his growing family to England. While living first in Wales and then England, Deeming and his wife had a son and another daughter. Deeming was soon up to old tricks and spent nine months in a Hull prison for forgery. While he was in prison, Marie was left to fend for herself with the children. She also suffered humiliation from Deeming's multiple affairs, which he conducted in the open.

Now out of prison, Deeming immediately took on a false identity. He rented the Dinham Villa in the village of Rainhill under the alias of *Albert Williams*. He brought his first wife, Marie, and their four children to the villa. Because he was now known as Williams, he said Marie was his sister visiting from Wales, and the children were his nieces and nephew when anyone asked.

Each night, Deeming would sit at the Rainhill pub and tell tales of his sea adventures to anyone who would listen. A frequent listener, Emily Mather, a young local woman, became infatuated with Deeming, and the two started dating. They became engaged, and then Deeming married her bigamously in February 1890. The marriage certificate said "Albert Williams, bachelor, and Emily Mather, spinster." Emily Mather was now Emily Williams, and she had no idea Deeming was a criminal who was already married with four children.

Deeming now had two wives and four children, and he decided that his first family had to go. On July 26th, 1891, Deeming viciously murdered Marie and their four children, slitting their throats and burying them in the floor of the Dinham Villa, where he then laid new concrete. He told those who asked that his sister and her children had returned to Wales. He lived at the villa with his new bride, who was unaware that his previous family was entombed underneath them.

BACK TO AUSTRALIA

Needing another fresh start, in November 1891, Frederick Deeming traveled by steamship to Australia with his new, unsuspecting wife, Emily. They arrived in Melbourne in December, where Deeming rented a cottage in the Melbourne suburb of Windsor under the name *Mr. Drewn*. However, after paying just one month's rent, Deeming left the property alone.

On Christmas Eve or in the early hours of Christmas Day in 1891, Deeming brutally murdered Emily Mather in their Windsor cottage. He slit her throat and buried her body under the hearthstone in one of the bedrooms. Deeming carefully covered Mather's remains with cement in an attempt to conceal his crime.

DREWN-WILLIAMS-DEEMING

By March, another family had moved into the Windsor cottage, and they complained to the landlord about a foul smell. Recognizing what it might be, the police were called to the property. The decomposing body of Emily Mather was discovered under the hearthstone. Police launched an investigation, quickly connecting the dots between *Mr. Drewn* and *Mr. Williams,* who arrived on the *Kaiser Wilhelm II* steamship, and Frederick Deeming. Interviews with fellow ship's passengers provided confirming descriptions of Deeming and Mather traveling together. An inquest held that officially determined that Emily Mather had been murdered, though Deeming's whereabouts were still unknown.

The newspapers covered the murder widely, which led to the arrest of Frederick Deeming in March 1892 in Western Australia, where he was now going by the name *Baron Swanston.* Deeming was identified by his physical description, including his long, wide mustache and the fact that he was carrying the marriage certificate from his marriage to Mather, along with several items that belonged to Emily, including her prayer book and a set of gloves. He had already proposed marriage to another woman named Kate Rounsefell, telling her "she would never regret it, and would always congratulate herself on having entered into matrimony with him." Rounsefell accepted the proposal, but the marriage was called off once Deeming was extradited to Melbourne to stand trial.

On his five-day train journey, Deeming was accompanied by three armed constables on his five-day train journey to Perth. The train made overnight stops in several towns, and Deeming struggled, fainting twice because he couldn't sleep or eat. Crowds and angry mobs gathered on the platform each day to catch a glimpse of Deeming, described by the newspapers as a handsome man with a distinctive, wide mustache and full head of hair. The guards maintained a vigilant watch over him, and he remained handcuffed at all times, except one night when he was taken into the town to sleep in a prison cell.

When the constables came to get him the following day, Deeming's large mustache had vanished. With the mustache gone, Deeming looked quite different. He had no access to a razor, but in the cell, guards discovered a small piece of a glass medicine bottle. Deeming had fashioned a makeshift razor from the small shard. He had also painstakingly pulled out about 75% of the mustache hairs from their roots.

The lead officer, Detective Cawsey, was upset by the transformation, recognizing how drastically it altered Deeming's appearance. He was also aware that eyewitness statements gathered for the prosecution mentioned the mustache. Deeming seemed pleased, and they continued on their journey to Perth.

THE FIRST FAMILY

Acting on information surrounding Mather's death in Australia, investigators in the English village of Rainhill dug under the concrete floor of Dinham Villa, the home Deeming had rented as "Albert Williams" in mid-1891. Buried beneath the stones were the decomposed bodies of Deeming's first wife, Marie, and his four young children — Bertha, Mary, Sidney, and baby Leala.

In 1892, a New Zealand paper, *Tuapeka Times*, wrote about the discovery of Marie Demming and the bodies of the Demming children.

"The house which had been occupied by the prisoner was entered and digging operations commenced in the kitchen, the floor of which had been cemented. After an hour's work, a horrible and sickening smell was encountered, which compelled the police to desist from their labor for a time. The first article found was a tablecloth and a woman's apron, and underneath these, the bodies of a woman and two children were found wrapped in oilcloth and Turkish toweling. In half an hour, two more bodies were dug out of the cement in which they were embedded. These were of a baby and a little girl. Of the five victims, the mother and one child had been strangled, while the other three children had their throats cut. The ages of the three older children appeared to be nine, seven, and five years respectively, while the baby seemed to be eighteen months. The mother appeared to be about thirty-five years of age. She was fully dressed in clothes of a superior description, and her body was tightly tied with a rope. The children were in their night-shirts."

An inquest into the Rainhill murders was held on March 18th, 1892. Deeming's brothers formally identified the bodies as Marie and the four Deeming children. The remains had lain there undiscovered for over eight months until the sensational news of Mather's murder in Australia led investigators to unravel Deeming's past crimes.

TRIAL AND EXECUTION

Deeming went on trial in April 1892 for Mather's murder and was defiant up to the end, trying to plead insanity. He claimed to have caught syphilis and had nightly visitations from his deceased mother's spirit, which told him to kill. He testified on the stand and tried to justify the murder of his wife and children in Rainhill in a long speech. He never admitted or confessed to the murder of his wife, Emily Mather, saying only that he thought she had run off with another man and wasn't dead.

The jury found him guilty after deliberating for just over an hour. Deeming spent his last days writing his autobiography and poetry in his cell up until his execution. The courts rejected his appeals.

On May 23rd, 1892, Deeming was hanged at Melbourne Gaol at 10:01 am as punishment for Mather's murder. He was 39 years old. Deeming showed no remorse for his crimes.

DOUBT

Darlie Routier has been on death row in Texas for 26 years. In 1997, when she was 27 years old, she was convicted and sentenced to death for the brutal murder of her five-year-old son, Damon. She was also charged with the murder of her six-year-old son Devon, who was killed in the same attack, though she has not yet been tried for his murder.

Routier, who is serving her sentence at the Mountain View Unit in Gatesville, Texas, maintains that she is innocent and that an intruder entered her home in Rowlett, Texas, attacked her, and stabbed her two young boys to death as they slept. Criminal professionals and amateur sleuths alike still debate this case.

On June 6th, 1996, Damon and Devon were stabbed repeatedly with a large kitchen knife as they lay on a couch in the family room. Routier herself sustained severe slash wounds and bruising to her neck and arms, which she claims were inflicted by the intruder.

During the attack, Routier's 7-month-old infant, Drake, and her husband, Darin, were unharmed upstairs.

In the chaos after the brutal attack, Darlie Routier called 911, screaming in a high-pitched voice, claiming an intruder had entered the home, murdered her sons, and attacked her before fleeing the house.

Partial transcript of the beginning of the call:

---

911 Operator: Rowlett 911. What is your emergency?

Darlie Routier: Somebody came here...they broke in!

911 Operator: Ma'am?

Darlie Routier: They just stabbed me and my children!

911 Operator: What?

Darlie Routier: They just stabbed me and my kids...my little boys...

911 Operator: Who? Who did?

Darlie Routier: My little boy is dying!

MINUTES AFTER THE ATTACK

Police arrived within minutes and found the floors and walls in the rec room splattered with blood. There were two young children dead or dying and a distraught mother with serious injuries.

The police discovered one of the home's window screens had been cut open, seemingly indicating a possible point of entry or exit. However, an immediate search of the house and grounds did not locate an intruder on the scene. Blood drops stopped in the utility room through which Routier said the intruder fled into the garage. With no intruder found, police focused on securing the scene and allowing medical personnel to assist the victims.

According to Routier's account, she fell asleep with her sons Devon and Damon while watching television in the rec room when the unknown intruder entered the home. Devon and Damon sustained multiple stab wounds inflicted by a large kitchen knife. According to the medical examiner, Devon was stabbed twice in the chest, which allowed blood to flow into his lungs. Damon was stabbed four times in the back, and his injuries would have allowed him to survive for only about eight minutes.

Routier herself had suffered severe slash wounds to her

neck and arms, and her forearms were bruised. She told police that the intruder was a white male dressed in black clothing, and he dropped the knife in the utility room as he ran. Routier said she picked up the knife and chased after him. Once she realized she and her boys had been seriously wounded, she called 911 within six minutes of the attack.

In her call with 911, Routier mentions the knife the perpetrator used three times.

Two minutes into the 911 call:

Darlie Routier: Some man came in, stabbed my babies, stabbed me. I woke up. I was fighting. He ran out through the garage...threw the knife down. My babies are dying. They're dead. Oh my God.

Four minutes into the 911 call:

Darlie Routier: Ya'll look out in the garage. Look out in the garage. They left a knife laying on...

911 Operator: There's a knife? Don't touch anything.

Darlie Routier: I already touched it and picked it up.

Five minutes into the 911 call:

911 Operator: (You) need to let the police officers in the front door.

Darlie Routier: … his knife was lying over there, and I already picked it up.

911 Operator: OK…it's alright …it's ok…

Darlie Routier: God. I bet if we could have gotten the prints, maybe …maybe…

The three victims were transported to Baylor Medical Center, and both boys were pronounced dead at the hospital. Routier had surgery and spent several days in the hospital recovering from her wounds. Police questioned her, and at times, her story differed. She thought, at one point, there may have been two intruders. During that time, she had the support of her family, friends, and the community, including her husband, Darin.

Damon and Devon were buried together, holding hands, and were interred in one grave. Devon would have turned seven years old 10 days after his murder. The local news aired footage of Routier spraying Silly String on her sons' tombstone and singing *Happy Birthday* at a morbid birthday party for Devon at the grave. Though intended as a quiet memorial, her smiles and laughter were seen as evidence of callousness. Supporters, however, pointed to an earlier somber ceremony that was not broadcast.

Routier expressed regret, saying she was trying to fulfill Devon's wishes after his life was cut short so tragically. The Routiers were known for giving lavish birthday parties for their children, and Routier thought this should be no exception.

The Routier family had a large home in Rowlett, Texas. The Colonial-style home with rooftop dormers and porch pillars was nicknamed the "Home Alone" house from the 1990 movie because of its size and luxury. Darin Routier had a tech supply company that had seen some success, although, in recent years, money had been tight. At the time of the murders, the Routiers had less than $2,000 on hand, and Darin had just been turned down for a $5,000 loan.

THE INVESTIGATION

In the first two weeks of the murder investigation, police found no physical evidence of an intruder. The window screen that had been cut was just that. There was no disturbance in the layers of dust around the window and no disturbance in the bark dust and dirt outside the window, which police would expect to see if an intruder entered or exited the home that way.

The police doubted that Routier would have slept through such a vicious assault on her children, especially since she was in the same room, and yet she allegedly slept through the stabbings and only awoke when she was attacked.

Crime scene analysts noted an absence of blood drops in the garage where Routier stated the offender exited. Yet, there were several blood drops in the utility room where Routier said the assailant dropped the knife, and she picked it up. Officers saw that the utility room sink appeared suspiciously clean. After they sprayed the area with Luminol and turned off the lights, the sink basin and countertop glowed with blood. Someone had cleaned up. While not visible, Luminol also revealed a small child's bloody handprint on the leather sofa in the rec room. Someone had tried to wipe it away.

Other than blood splatter, the rec room showed little sign of a struggle. A lampshade was askew, fresh flowers were on the floor, and the police thought they looked like they had been placed there rather than thrown. A vacuum cleaner lay on its side, yet there was blood on the carpet underneath the vacuum, so it had fallen or been pushed over after someone had been stabbed. Routier's purse and wallet were in the rec room, and nothing was missing.

A bloody sock was discovered 75 yards from the home. Analysis of the sock showed it contained blood from both murdered boys, yet there was no other blood evidence outside.

Two weeks after the murders, the police asked Darin and Darlie to come to the station for another interview. They were placed in separate rooms and questioned.

After the questions, Darlie Routier was arrested and charged with the murder of her five-year-old son Damon. The charge of murdering a child five years or under carried the death penalty if convicted, and while Routier was later charged with Devon's murder, the prosecutor intended to try Routier for capital murder.

THE TRIAL

The prosecution portrayed Routier as a selfish and materialistic woman who killed her children due to the family's financial difficulties. They argued she staged the crime scene to point blame at an imaginary intruder. The infamous "Silly String" video was shown to jurors, depicting a smiling Routier spraying the graves of her dead sons in celebration of what would have been Devon's 7th birthday.

The defense asserted there was no discernible motive for Routier to murder her children. They highlighted the lack of any confession or eyewitnesses and portrayed Routier as a doting mother who loved her family. They said she had no time to stage an elaborate crime scene in the short timeframe before paramedics arrived. Her slash wounds came within millimeters of severing her carotid artery and were unlikely to be self-inflicted. With her surviving son upstairs, they questioned why she would spare him yet brutally kill Devon and Damon.

MEDICAL PERSONNEL

Many medical personnel who cared for Routier at Baylor Medical Center were asked to testify at her trial. The testimonies offered during the trial were often at odds with the notes recorded in Routier's medical records from her time at the hospital.

On June 6th, the medical records reported Routier's family was by her side throughout the day. One note specifically urged the family to allow the patient to rest and to refrain from discussing the assault and murders. It was also noted that Routier was regularly administered pain medication and sometimes anti-anxiety medication. Some of her statements to the police regarding her home intrusion and the subsequent attacks on her and her children were made under the influence of these medications.

Dr. Patrick Dillawn was on duty when Routier was admitted to the emergency department on June 6th. On the stand, Dr. Dillawn described Routier as agitated by the police presence but not particularly upset otherwise. He remembered her shedding a few tears at the sight of her children's photograph. However, this was inconsistent with his own notes, which described Routier as "tearful" and "frightened.".

Jody Fitts, a registered nurse at Baylor Medical Center in June of 1996, remembered the early morning hours when Routier was first admitted. She testified that Routier was hysterical, screaming, and covered in dried blood. Fitts also recalled removing a necklace that was embedded in her neck wound.

Jody Cotner, a trauma nurse at Baylor, recalled meeting Routier in the ICU. She downplayed her emotional state, suggesting she wasn't grieving as a mother normally would. However, during cross-examination, she admitted that she hadn't taken any notes on Routier's behavior.

Diane Hollon, another nurse at Baylor, testified that Routier didn't show much emotion, although she did become tearful when looking at her boys' pictures. However, this contradicted the medical chart notes she wrote, which described her as "very emotional" and having "periods of crying/sobbing."

Paige Campbell testified for the prosecution, claiming she never saw a tear run down Routier's face. However, this was at odds with her own notes that described her as "very tearful."

Another Baylor nurse, Denise Faulk, recalled that Routier was not crying when she recounted the attack. But, in contradiction, her notes stated that the patient was "tearful at times."

Much debate centered around the bloody sock found 75 yards from the home. While the prosecution alleged

Routier planted it to falsely implicate an intruder, the defense contended it supported her story, proving the perpetrator fled the scene.

Routier took the stand despite advice not to do so. She read passages from her diary discussing how much she loved her sons and prayed for them. She also read entries that discussed her mental health. She felt depressed and had talked about taking sleeping pills to attempt suicide with her husband, Darin. Her cross-examination by the prosecution was brutal. She struggled to answer questions and was reduced to tears on the stand.

In the end, on February 1st, 1997, the jury deliberated for four hours and found Routier guilty of killing her 5-year-old son. Three days later, she was sentenced to death by lethal injection.

POST-TRIAL

Following Darlie Routier's conviction, her defense team worked diligently to identify potential errors or oversights during the murder investigation and trial. They felt strongly that the whole truth had not yet come to light.

Her attorneys began assembling an appeal based on multiple alleged mistakes and oversights. From their standpoint, the analysis of the murder scene was critically flawed, especially given the limited timeframe in which Routier would have had to stage the elaborate crime. Her lawyers also pointed to discrepancies in the official court transcript that undermined her right to a fair trial. Once analyzed, the court transcript contained approximately 33,000 mistakes. The jury was also not shown the bruising that Routier had on both her fore-arms, which they felt proved she struggled with some-one. Despite their passionate claims, initial appeals were denied by the courts. Routier was finally able to appeal her conviction in 2001, but it was upheld in 2003.

In 2008, more than a decade after her sons' deaths, Routier was granted the right to pursue advanced DNA testing that was unavailable at the time of the original investigation. This provided a glimmer of hope that new evidence could emerge to support her continued claims of innocence. Her case was sent back to the state court system to allow for additional forensic analysis.

In January 2014, both prosecution and defense supported a new round of DNA testing on several crit-ical pieces of evidence, including a bloody fingerprint found at the scene and the controversial sock found 75 yards from the home. The fingerprint yielded no matches.

In 2018, the court authorized a third battery of DNA tests, again with the agreement of both sides. As tech-nology improves, her attorneys remain hopeful that DNA results will exonerate her once and for all. Until those findings are revealed, the painful fight goes on for Routier and all those convinced of her innocence.

Over two decades later, Routier maintains that she was wrongfully convicted of this devastating crime. Routier and her husband eventually divorced, but he has always maintained her innocence.

NO ESCAPE

On August 8th, 2015, a tragic family shooting occurred inside a home in Harris County, Texas, near Houston. The perpetrator of this violence was 48-year-old David Ray Conley III. Conley had broken into the house of his ex-girlfriend, Valerie Jackson. Valerie Conley had lived together off and on for several years, and Conley had fathered two of her children, Natalie and Nathaniel Conley. Still, their relationship had ended after several domestic violence incidents, and Valerie had changed the door locks. Undeterred, Conley found an unlocked window and let himself into the home.

Valerie Jackson lived on Falling Oaks Road with her husband, Dwayne Jackson, Sr., age 50, and their six children. On the day of the murders, David Conley's 13-year-old son Nathaniel was home. Once inside, Conley immediately confronted Valerie Jackson, her husband Dwayne, and the children. Brandishing a 9mm handgun, he herded the panicked family into the main bedroom at gunpoint. Conley began binding and restraining the victims by tying them up or handcuffing them.

While Conley was distracted, Valerie Jackson secretly texted her mother, telling her that Conley had shown up with a gun and was holding them hostage. Soon after sending the text, the horrific events of the next nine hours began. Throughout the afternoon and evening, Conley systematically shot each family member in the back of the head, forcing Valerie to witness the killings of her husband and children. She was the last victim, left alive until all others had been murdered.

NO RESCUE

As the slaughter occurred inside the home, police were called repeatedly to perform welfare checks on the residence. The first occurred around 10:42 am after Valerie's mother received her panicked text and contacted the authorities. Officers arrived and checked outside the house but received no response from within. They returned once more during the afternoon after concerned family members also expressed worry to police dispatchers. Yet on both occasions, the officers found no signs of distress at the residence and left having seen no visible threats. They had no idea the family members were being shot with each passing hour.

As the Saturday afternoon wore on inside the sweltering house, Conley began pulling his victims from their bindings one by one. He spun each struggling captive to face away from him, pressing the cold metal of the gun against their head before he squeezed the trigger, ending their life with a single gunshot to the back of the head. The children Jonah Jackson, 6; Trinity Jackson, 7; Caleb Jackson, 9; Dwayne Jackson Jr., 10; Honesty Jackson, 11; Nathaniel Conley, 13, were murdered first, followed by Valerie's husband, Dwayne. By late evening, only Valerie and Conley remained in the house, and with the pull of the trigger, Conley shot 40-year-old Valorie, and the massacre was complete. The Jackson family were now all deceased, including Nathaniel, David Conley's own son.

Officers were called to the house a third time, and this time, one of the officers peered through a window and spotted a boy lying in a pool of blood. The officers tried to access the house, but Conley shot at them. They quickly pulled back and awaited reinforcements. A negotiator was brought in to talk to Conley. During their conversation, Conley confessed to shooting Valorie, Dwayne, and the children. Conley also spoke with his daughter Natalie on the phone, revealing that he had killed her mother, her brother Nathaniel, and her step-siblings.

Conley finally gave up and was arrested after a tense standoff with police. He was charged with three counts of capital murder. At his initial court appearance, Conley sat silently as the judge denied him bail. He was remanded to the Harris County Jail to await his fate.

On August 17th, over 200 people gathered at Fallbrook Church in northwest Houston to honor the lives of the Jackson family. As the bodies of Valerie Jackson and her loved ones were laid to rest, the legal process against David Conley soon began.

THE OFF AND ON RELATIONSHIP

Conley had a long history of violence with Valerie Jackson, and domestic incidents leading to prison time were usually responsible for their many break-ups. However, Valerie had dated and had children with Dwayne Jackson over the years, which became a consistent point of aggravation for David Conley.

In 2013, Conley served a nine-month prison sentence for a family-related assault. Surprisingly, that same year, Jackson praised him as the "best father in the whole world" on her Facebook.

Valerie Jackson affectionately called Conley "My baby, my best friend, my forever." She expressed gratitude for him prioritizing their family and maintaining their home. "We love you, David Ray Conley III!" she posted.

After his release from prison, Jackson remained optimistic about their relationship, sharing light-hearted moments on social media. "Lucky to be married to someone like (MacGyver). I think he diagnosed the issue with my washing machine."

However, their relationship took a wrong turn when Conley assaulted Valerie. According to sources in the family, Valerie had attempted to grab a belt from him, resulting in her being forcefully slammed against a refrigerator. Authorities believe he intended to use the belt on Dwayne Jackson Jr. as a disciplinary measure. Conley left and moved into a motel, and a warrant was issued for his arrest after Valerie decided to file charges.

According to those closest to him, Conley struggled with bipolar disorder and mental instability and consistently used claims of mental illness to excuse his wrongdoings.

Conley did an interview from jail with the local ABC news station and gave this answer when asked why he murdered the Jacksons and his own child.

"Nate didn't give me any respect because of what his mother was doing towards me. She ignored me. I understand, like you said, all these people are dead, but Valerie wasn't a Good Samaritan. They (she and Dwayne Jackson) did evil stuff all the time. I was doing my part as God asked me to do. God asked me to help them. God says in the Bible thou shall not disrespect thy mother and thy father. I'm highly spiritual. I'm not crazy. I'm not like that."

Conley told the reporter that the children were growing up to be monsters.

During another interview with the Houston Chronicle, Conley said Dwayne Jackson was a bully and was teaching the kids bullying.

"He's a demon. He was a bad person. He (was) not on God's side. He threw a brick through my van window. He never bought the kids nothing."

PROSECUTION AND TRIAL

Prosecutors announced their intention to pursue the death penalty against Conley for his monstrous crimes. As the months dragged on, Conley's defense attorneys indicated he was not culpable due to his alleged mental deficiencies. A psychologist would later deem him disabled, though this did little to assuage the community's anger over the murders.

After six years of legal proceedings, a resolution was finally reached. In October 2021, Conley was convicted at trial for the killings. Rather than face a jury's sentence of death, however, prosecutors acknowledged Conley's alleged disability and agreed to life in prison without the possibility of parole.

A MURDER STORY

Retired teacher and adoptee Kathy Gillcrist waited until she was close to sixty years old before seeking out her birth family. Growing up, she had no curiosity to know who her birth parents were or if she had other siblings. In retirement, she decided it would be an exciting project to tackle. She took a DNA test and waited for the results to come back. After looking at all her genetic "cousins," she contacted her third cousin, who was an amateur genealogist and asked for help.

After months of research, her cousin found her parents. While there was nothing particularly remarkable about her birthmother other than a liaison with her birthfather in 1956, her birthfather was a different story.

He was an accomplished, educated American diplomat who murdered his entire family in 1976 and escaped. The first picture she saw of him was an FBI "most wanted list" mugshot with the heading, "wanted for unlawful flight to avoid persecution and murder with a blunt instrument."

The family likeness was undeniable. They had the same nose, mouth, and dimpled chin. They even shared a mole in the same spot on their face.

Kathy finally had the story of her parents. They were never married, and her mother was young and gave her up for adoption. Gillcrist's birth father may not have even known of her existence, as the family he created and murdered was after her birth in 1957. Her father's background intrigued her, and as her story surfaced in the local media, she was contacted by officials and other people connected with the case. She was shocked to discover that her father was only 21 when she was born. William Bishop could still be alive.

William Bradford Bishop Jr. was born on August 1st, 1936, in Pasadena, California, to Lobelia Amaryllis St. Germain and William Bradford Bishop Sr. He attended South Pasadena High School and went on to earn a bachelor's degree in history from Yale University as well as a master's degree in international studies from Middlebury College. Bishop also held a master's degree in African Studies from UCLA.

After graduating from Yale in 1959, Bishop married Annette Weis, his high school sweetheart, and then had three sons. He joined the United States Army and spent four years working in counterintelligence. Bishop was fluent in five languages: English, Italian, French, Spanish and Serbo-Croatian. After leaving the Army, he joined the U.S. State Department and served in the Foreign Service with numerous overseas postings. His family accompanied him on these postings. This included postings in the Italian cities of Verona, Milan, and Florence from 1968 to 1972, where he did postgraduate work at the University of Florence. He also served in Africa, with posts in Ethiopia and Botswana, from 1972 to 1974.

Bishop's final posting in 1974 was at the State Department in Washington, D.C. At the time, he was living in Bethesda, Maryland, with his wife, three sons, and his mother, Lobelia.

On March 1st, 1976, after learning he would not receive the promotion he had sought at the State Department, Bishop told his secretary that he was feeling unwell and left his office. This was the last confirmed sighting of Bishop by his colleague Roy Harrell, who noted that Bishop seemed agitated.

THE MURDER PLAN

Police believe Bishop drove to his bank, where he withdrew several hundred dollars before going to the Montgomery Mall. At the mall, he purchased a ball-peen hammer and gas can, which he used to fill up the can and the tank of his 1974 Chevrolet station wagon at a nearby gas station. Bishop then went to a hardware store to buy a shovel and pitchfork.

Between 7:30 and 8:00 pm, Bishop returned to his home in Bethesda. His wife, Annette, was likely killed first, followed by his mother, Lobelia, when she returned from walking the family dog. Finally, Bishop went upstairs and killed his three sleeping sons, Geoffrey, age 5, Brent, age 10, and Brad III, age 14. Bishop then loaded the bodies into the station wagon and drove 275 miles to a densely wooded area about 5 miles south of Columbia, North Carolina.

On March 2nd, Bishop dug a shallow hole and piled the bodies inside before dousing them with gasoline and setting them on fire. Discovered along with the burned bodies were a gas can, pitchfork, and shovel with a label from Poch's Hardware store.

Later that same day, Bishop was known to have purchased items at a sporting goods store in Jacksonville, North Carolina. According to witnesses, he had the family dog with him and may have been accompanied by an unidentified woman described only as "dark-skinned."

On March 10th, 1976, a neighbor who had not seen the Bishop family for some time contacted the police to do a welfare check. A detective was sent to the home, where he found blood on the front porch, floor, walls, and bedrooms.

Officers didn't realize that the bodies of the Bishop family had already been found in North Carolina on March 2nd. Forest Ranger Ronald Brickhouse discovered the bodies of the family after a fire spotter had reported smoke from a watchtower.

The bodies of Annette and her mother-in-law, Lobelia, were lying on top of the three boys. The women wore street clothes, and the boys were in pajamas. Each victim had a bloody towel wrapped around their head. The medical examiner said all had been beaten to death with a blunt instrument. Dental records later confirmed that the burned bodies discovered in North Carolina belonged to Bishop's wife, mother, and three sons.

ON THE RUN

On March 18th, Bishop's abandoned 1974 Chevrolet station wagon was found at an isolated campground in Elkmont, Tennessee. The car was located in Great Smoky Mountains National Park, just a few miles from the Appalachian Trail and about 400 miles from where the bodies had been buried in North Carolina. Authorities found dog biscuits, a bloody blanket, a shotgun, an ax, and a shaving kit containing Bishop's medication inside the car. The trunk's spare tire well was filled with blood. Based on witness statements, it was determined the car had been there for about two weeks.

"I have always held the theory that that car was placed in that location as a ruse. Bradford Bishop could be somewhere over at Chapel Hill with a beard walking around. Bradford Bishop, with his background, is capable of doing that..."

RUFUS EDMISTEN, NORTH CAROLINA ATTORNEY GENERAL, *THE CHARLOTTE OBSERVER*, APRIL 28TH, 1976

Police theorized that after abandoning the car, Bishop likely joined hikers on the Appalachian Trail in an attempt to disappear. However, attempts to track him using bloodhounds were unsuccessful. The next day, on March 19, 1976, a grand jury indicted Bishop on five counts of first-degree murder.

Bishop's motives for murdering his family have never been fully explained. Although Bishop had been passed over for a promotion, he had no history of problems at work and had had a successful career.

MOTIVE SPECULATION

It was reported that Bishop frequently faced criticism from his wife, Annette, age 37, and mother, Lobelia, age 68, over his lack of advancement at the State Department. Bishop was said to be unhappy with his desk job and wanted a foreign posting, but his wife was reluctant to move abroad again. Annette had started taking art classes at the University of Maryland despite Bishop wanting her to remain a stay-at-home mother.

Most sources agree the Bishops had some financial issues, but the extent is unclear. Some described them as mild and typical, while others reported the IRS was auditing the family due to money troubles.

Bishop had a history of depression and insomnia, for which he took medications. He was an avid outdoorsman who enjoyed camping and hiking. Bishop was also fond of dogs, scotch whiskey, and spicy foods. He had a six-inch surgical scar on his lower back, cleft chin, and facial mole. Bishop likely took his father's revolver and Yale class ring when he disappeared. Authorities believe he also took his diplomatic passport to avoid detection.

SIGHTINGS

In the over 40 years since the murders, there have been

numerous reported sightings of Bishop across Europe, including Sweden, Italy, Belgium, England, Finland, the Netherlands, Germany, Greece, Spain, and Switzerland.

In July 1978, a Swedish woman who had worked with Bishop in Ethiopia claimed she saw him twice in one week at a public park in Stockholm. She did not contact the police at the time because she was unaware he was a wanted fugitive.

In January 1979, Bishop's former State Department colleague Roy Harrell reported seeing him in a restaurant restroom in Sorrento, Italy. When Harrell addressed the bearded man as Bishop, he denied his identity and quickly fled.

On September 19th, 1994, a former neighbor who knew the Bishops in Bethesda claimed to see Bishop up close on a train platform in Basel, Switzerland. She described him as well-groomed and said he later got into a car at the station.

Bishop's case has been featured extensively in media and television shows in recent decades. In 2010, authorities believed he likely lived in plain sight somewhere in Europe or California, possibly working as a teacher or involved in criminal activities.

Before the murders, Bishop had been corresponding with an Illinois federal prison inmate named Albert

Kenneth Bankston for unknown reasons. Bankston died in 1983 without knowing of the murders or that Bishop was wanted.

In 2014, the FBI exhumed a John Doe killed in a 1981 Alabama car accident after speculation he could have been Bishop. However, DNA testing confirmed the man's identity was not a match. Authorities now believe Bishop resides in the U.S., and he avoids arrest to prevent his identification through fingerprints.

THE SEARCH CONTINUES

Forensic artist Karen Taylor created an age progression sculpture at the FBI's request to suggest what Bishop may look like around age 77. Using this sculpture, images were made showing Bishop with possible facial hair and glasses as disguises.

In early April 2014, WRC-TV in Washington D.C. launched a website displaying extensive information about the case, including samples of Bishop's handwriting, fingerprints, dental records, and previously unseen family videos.

The latest information in the case came from the positive DNA test from Kathy Gillcrist. It's possible that Bishop has had other children after murdering his family, and they may show up in databases as well.

While Bishop has managed to avoid capture for over forty years, the confirmation he is likely still alive has energized law enforcement efforts. Authorities believe it is only a matter of time before he is finally arrested and made to answer for his crimes, even as an octogenarian.

FROM KILLER CASE FILES: SERIAL POLICEMAN

"Schaefer is the most sexually deviant person I had ever seen. He made Ted Bundy look like a Boy Scout."

PROSECUTOR ROBERT STONE

Nestled within the Sunshine State, Martin County, Florida, is known for its awe-inspiring landscapes, sandy beaches, and its year-round temperate weather. In the 1970s, droves of young people from across the United States were attracted to this idyllic corner of the state, nicknamed the Treasure Coast. Little did they know a serial killer wearing a cop's uniform lurked among them.

A KILLER IS BORN

Gerard John Schaefer Jr. was born on March 26th, 1946, in the quaint town of Neenah, Wisconsin. He was the firstborn and had two younger sisters. His father, Gerard Sr., made a living as a traveling salesman, while his mother, Doris Marie, spent her time caring for the children at home. The family frequently relocated before ultimately settling down in Fort Lauderdale, Florida, in 1960.

The Schaefer family had money and frequented the local yachting and country clubs. They kept up appearances, but the family was dysfunctional. Schaefer's father was an alcoholic who routinely subjected Doris Marie and the children to verbal abuse. Despite his frequent absences, he showed little affection for his son, instead favoring his daughters, which fueled Schaefer's jealousy. Schaefer remained deeply attached to his mother as a child, but he eventually felt like neither of his parents cared for him.

DARK DESIRES

While at St. Thomas Aquinas High School, Schaefer was somewhat of a loner, keeping to himself and having few friends. He was fond of solitary activities such as hunting, fishing, and immersing himself in the natural world. On these outings, he would tie himself to trees and fantasize about dying because it sexually excited him.

While in high school, he had a girlfriend, Cindy, who participated in his "rape fantasies." She broke up with him after three years.

Schaefer continued to pursue his fantasies that revolved around bondage and sadomasochism. He was frequently seen peering through windows in his neighborhood and even broke into some homes to steal women's underwear. He began cross-dressing while still in high school, although he later said this was to avoid being drafted into the Vietnam War.

After graduating in June 1964, he enrolled at Broward Community College in the Fall, where he pursued a teaching degree. In 1968, Schaefer received a scholarship to attend Florida Atlantic University in Boca Raton.

A SERIES OF FAILURES

In December 1968, Schaefer married Martha Louise Fogg, a woman two years his junior. Their marriage didn't last long and ended on May 2nd, 1970. Fogg cited Schaefer's excessive demands for sex and extreme cruelty as reasons for the divorce.

Schaefer started teaching in March 1969, but he was dismissed from two schools within two years due to unprofessional behavior and insufficient knowledge of his subjects. Schaefer took some time off after his dismissal and traveled through Europe and North Africa before returning to Florida.

He applied to become a police officer at the Wilton Manors Police Department. Even though Schaefer failed the psychological part of his police exam, he was officially appointed a patrolman for Broward County in September 1971. That same month, Schaefer married his second wife, Teresa Dean.

Schaefer's tenure at the Broward County Police Department lasted six months. He was fired when it was discovered that he regularly stopped female drivers, recorded their license plates, and contacted them to arrange sexual encounters.

Remarkably, his career in law enforcement continued. Schaefer became a deputy at the Martin County Sheriff's Department. He provided a counterfeit letter of recommendation, and since his record showed no previous convictions, he was hired by Martin County in June 1972.

THE ABDUCTION OF NANCY AND PAULA

On July 21st, 1972, Gerard Schaefer, while on duty, encountered two hitchhiking teenage girls, Nancy Trotter, and Paula Wells. He escorted them back to their lodging in Stuart, where he lectured them on the perils of hitchhiking, even falsely claiming hitchhiking was illegal in Martin County. When the girls discussed their plans to visit the beach the following day, Schaefer offered to drive them there.

The next day, Nancy and Paula met Schaefer on East Ocean Boulevard around 9 am. Rather than driving the girls to the beach as promised, Schaefer took them to Hutchinson Island, all the while continuing to lecture them about the dangers of hitchhiking. He stopped the vehicle and threatened the girls with his gun. Schaefer led them into a thickly wooded area after handcuffing them. He separated them, tying each girl to a different tree, and he placed nooses he'd made around their necks. They stood precariously on exposed tree roots, and any wrong step or attempt to escape would result in their deaths.

Unexpectedly, Schaefer received a radio dispatch summoning him to the police station. He told the girls that he would return shortly and warned them not to try and escape. Ignoring his threats, both Nancy and Paula desperately worked to free themselves. It was dark, and they couldn't see each other in the dense forest. They went their separate ways upon escaping. Paula managed to reach the highway, where a truck driver stopped to assist her. He brought her to a nearby police station — the very one where Schaefer worked. Nancy was soon found near a creek with her hands still bound behind her back. Upon learning that Paula was safe, she was overcome with relief.

Schaefer returned to the forest two hours later only to find the girls had escaped. Panicked, he contacted his boss, Sheriff Robert Crowder, and confessed to tying up the girls in the woods to teach them a lesson about hitchhiking.

At the station, Nancy and Paula recounted their harrowing ordeal, describing their abductor and detailing their escape. They identified Gerard Schaefer as the man who had tied them to a tree in the forest and threatened to sexually assault and murder them.

Despite Schaefer's insistence on trying to scare the girls, his boss wasn't convinced. He was immediately fired, arrested, and charged with false imprisonment and aggravated assault. Schaefer spent two weeks in jail before posting bail. He found work at a Kwik Chek minute mart and awaited his trial, scheduled for November 1972.

In September 1972, Schaefer enrolled in classes at an adult education center in Fort Lauderdale under the alias Jerry Shepherd. There, he befriended 17-year-old Susan Place and 16-year-old Georgia Jessup. The teenagers were captivated by their new acquaintance, who claimed to have traveled extensively and harbored an interest in the supernatural. On September 27th, 1972, Susan's mother, Lucille, discovered her daughter hurriedly packing her belongings. Susan explained that she intended to accompany Georgia on a road trip with their friend Jerry.

Lucille briefly spoke with Jerry outside her home and also noted the license plate number of Jerry's 1969 Datsun. She bid her daughter farewell, and Susan assured her mother that they would stay in touch. After four days without contact from Susan, she and Georgia's mother reported the teenagers missing to the Oakland Park police. Although Lucille provided the license plate number, the investigation stalled due to incorrect jurisdiction.

THE FIRST TRIAL

In November 1972, Gerard Schaefer accepted a plea deal that reduced his sentence. Pleading guilty to aggravated assault, he was given a one-year sentence in county jail, with eligibility for parole after six months. Schaefer requested that the judge postpone his sentencing for a few weeks so he could help his wife, Teresa, relocate to Fort Lauderdale. Teresa wished to live closer to Schaefer's mother while he was in jail. The judge granted the request, given Schaefer's status as a police officer with no prior convictions. Schaefer remained free until January 15th, 1973, when he began serving his sentence in Martin County jail.

CONNECTING THE DOTS

In March 1973, Lucille Place, Susan's mother, discovered a letter sent by Jerry Shepherd (Schaefer's alias) in Susan's bedroom. Hoping to find her daughter, whom she still believed had run away, Lucille and her husband, Ira, drove to the address in Stuart, Florida. There, they learned that Jerry Shepherd was an alias used by Gerard Schaefer, who had been in jail since January for abducting two teenage girls. Realizing the connection between Schaefer and the disappearance of Susan and Georgia, Lucille contacted the police.

DISCOVERY OF THE BODIES

On April 1st, 1973, two men stumbled upon human remains in a shallow grave in Oak Hammock Park in Port Saint Lucie. The police were contacted, and the bodies were identified as Susan Place and Georgia Jessup. Both girls had been decapitated, and their bodies had been mutilated. They were found only six miles from where Schaefer had abducted Nancy Trotter and Paula Wells in July 1972. Given the similarities between the cases, investigators obtained search warrants for Schaefer's residence and his mother's house.

The search uncovered various weapons, Schaefer's "fictional" stories detailing kidnappings, sexual assaults, and hangings, over 30 Polaroid photos of mutilated women, and a box of items or trophies he'd taken from his victims. Most of the items were jewelry and teeth. This evidence linked Schaefer to several disappearances and murders. On May 18th, 1973, Schaefer was charged with the first-degree murder of Susan Place and Georgia Jessup and was sent for a psychiatric examination.

THE SECOND TRIAL

In September 1973, Schaefer's second trial began in St. Lucie County. Teresa Dean, Schaefer's wife, was initially unaware of her husband's crimes, but she became suspicious when he was fired from the police force. She testified against him at his trial. Her testimony focused on a photo album containing pictures of women in bondage and torture poses in their home.

The prosecution presented evidence of the gruesome double murder, while the defense attempted to prove that Susan Place's parents had identified the wrong person. After five hours of deliberation, the jury found Schaefer guilty of two counts of first-degree murder, and the judge sentenced him to two terms of life in prison.

Teresa Dean divorced her husband after the trial and refused to speak about their relationship.

HOW MANY WOMEN DID HE KILL?

The exact number of Schaefer's victims remains unknown, but the police compiled a list of potential victims after searching his homes. It is also unclear when Schaefer began killing women.

The first murder that can be connected to Schaefer was Leigh Farrell Hainline Bonadies, who disappeared on

September 8th, 1969. Other potential victims include Carmen Marie Hallock, Bonnie Taylor, Mary Alice Briscolina, and Elsie Lina Fermer.

Four years after the trial for the double murder, a set of bones and teeth belonging to Barbara Ann Wilcox and Colette Goodenough were found. The two teenagers from Iowa had been missing since 1973.

The bodies were found by a hog hunter near the C-24 Canal located in western Port St. Lucie. The girls had last been seen in Mississippi, hitchhiking to the east coast of Florida. The remains of the girls were discovered scattered around a large tree, and investigators' reports indicate that the tree showed signs of being used to hang one or both of the girls. According to the reports, an orange crate was found nearby, as if it had been used as a seat for a spectator. Although Schaefer was considered a likely suspect, the case remains unresolved.

SUZANNE GALE POOLE

The remains of a young female, later identified as Suzanne Gale Poole, who was also referred to as "Singer Island Jane Doe," were found by the Palm Beach County Sheriff's Office in a swampy area on Singer Island in June 1974. Suzanne had been tied to mangrove trees with wire. Despite numerous attempts to identify her over the years, including the development of a DNA profile for CODIS in 2015 and facial reconstruction in 2019, prior attempts had been unsuccessful.

In December 2021, the Sheriff's Office sent the remains to Othram Labs for genetic genealogy analysis for new leads. In March 2022, the in-house genealogy team at Othram found potential family members. The breakthrough came on June 2nd, 2022, when the young girl was identified as 15-year-old Suzanne "Susan" Gale Poole, who had been reported missing in 1972, just before Christmas.

Authorities believe that Poole was a victim of Gerald John Schaefer, and they are conducting further investigations to hopefully provide closure for Poole's family.

PRISON LIFE

While in prison, Schaefer relied heavily on mail to communicate with the outside world, and he wrote stories that often included murders. Schaefer was an avid writer, both before and after his arrest. His writings included graphic accounts of his crimes, as well as numerous fictional stories that contained similarly disturbing content. He also wrote letters to various individuals while in prison, including other known serial killers and true crime authors. He also helped the police break a child pornography ring from inside the prison in 1983.

Schaefer was mistrusted by fellow prisoners, who suspected he was an informant for the police. On December 3rd, 1995, Gerard Schaefer was stabbed to death in his cell by fellow inmate Vincent Faustino Rivera. Rivera stabbed Schaefer 43 times with a home-made shank. The motive for the murder remains unclear, though some suspect it was related to Schaefer's cooperation with the police. Other inmates reported that Rivera was also angry with Schaefer for taking two cups of hot water instead of one from the water fountain.

Rivera, already serving a life sentence, was found guilty of Schaefer's murder and received an additional 53 years and 10 months to his sentence.

Despite his brutal end and the mounting evidence against him, Gerard Schaefer continued to maintain his innocence, leaving the true scope of his crimes shrouded in mystery.

GET A FREE BOOK, AND MORE . . .

1. **Did you enjoy Family Annihilators?**

The #1 thing you can do to help me is to leave a review. Reviews elevate visibility and help new readers find all my books. Please consider leaving a review. I would really appreciate it!

2. **Don't forget to grab your free book!**

As a thank you to my readers, I created a special volume of my other series *Killer Case Files: 20 All New True Crime Stories.* You can download it right now for FREE in e-book or audio format at this link. https://dl.book funnel.com/tf4q1gethc

3. Would you like to join my **Launch Team** and receive a free volume before it's published?

If you are a reviewer on any of the well-known platforms like Amazon, Goodreads, or Instagram, you could receive an advance review copy of my future volumes. I'd love to have you on my official launch team!

More Info Here

4. To see all of my books - including multi-volume bundles and boxed sets - visit my Amazon author page here. My Author Page

5. Start Reading my *Killer Case Files: 100 Shocking Stories of Murder and Mayhem* bundle right here!

Killer Case Files Bundle

Thank you for being a reader.

Sincerely,

Jamie Malton

ABOUT THE AUTHORS

Jamie Malton is an award-winning, American, non-fiction writer. She is the author of Killer Case Files: Jamie Malton's Best True Crime Series which is an anthology of crime stories where the author examines the homicides perpetrated by murderers and serial killers.

Drawn to the how and why of real crime stories and fascinated by the detailed police work, DNA reconstruction, and genetic genealogy, she started writing her books to share the details of these stories with her readers.

For book research, she splits her time between the USA and European destinations, where she often visits some of the places where crimes have occurred.

With criminal apprehension and victim restitution as a personal cause, she donates a portion of her book sales to charities that fund DNA reconstruction to solve cold cases and charities that support the families of murdered victims.

You can reach her at JamieMalton.com.

AIDEN GALWAY

Aiden Galway is an author with an insatiable curiosity for unraveling the mysteries of the human psyche. He's particularly interested in disappearances, unsolved crimes, peculiar histories, and unexplained mysteries.

Born and raised in County Donegal, Ireland, Aiden's passion for storytelling started at an early age. Aiden's goal as a true crime writer is to shed light on heinous acts and explore the motivations that drive individuals to commit them.

Printed in Great Britain
by Amazon